justgrillthis

yum.

justgrillthis
SAM THE COOKING GUY

WILEY

JOHN WILEY & SONS, INC.

Library of Congress Cataloging-in-Publication Data

Zien, Sam.

Sam the Cooking Guy : just grill this / Sam Zien.

p. cm.

Includes index.

ISBN 978-0-470-46793-0 (pbk.)

1. Barbecue cookery. I. Title.

TX840.B3Z54 2011

641.7'6--dc22

2010016919

Printed in the United States of America

10 9 8 7 6 5 4 3 2 1

Cooking is like riding a bike—
the more you do it, the better you get.

—*Sam*

contents.

thank you's

Thank You's

My wife Kelly—I love you more than you know, but you are easily my absolute, no question, total food opposite. And now that I think of it, you're pretty much my complete opposite in everything. Turns out whoever wrote that thing about opposites attracting was absolutely right. I love you.

My boys—I love you all the days. I do owe Max an apology for being called "May" in the last book. But it wasn't my fault, it was my publisher's fault.

Justin—My friend and my voice of reason in the craziness of this process.

Gypsy—You always have my back, and I'm grateful for that.

Erin—For taking such good care of me

Steve—Get outta your Facebook, dude. You are the man.

Amy—Of course.

To Joan, Hailey, Emily, Max and Sophia, because you're all special — thanks.

My mom—Who I talk food with almost every day. I might look like Dad, but I am all you.

introduction.

delish.

isn't grilling simple anymore? What happened? When did it go from basic to ridiculously over the top? We're nothing if we don't have a Grillinator 6000 Titanium BBQ with Dual Source Infrared Heat capability (all for the suggested retail price of $12,500, use at your own risk, grill cover not included).

Because if you think about it, grilling really is the most fundamental of all cooking methods—a little heat and you're good. As simple as rubbing two sticks together . . . striking some flint against a rock, or using a magnifying glass to start a little fire. But noooo, someone had to go and change all that and make it complicated—not to mention making us feel inadequate at the same time.

So I want you to think of a grill as merely an oven and stove—that's outdoors. That's all it is.

Food cooked outside just tastes different than food cooked inside. Not necessarily better—just different. Okay, sometimes better. In fact, sometimes a lot better. Plus, there's just something wonderful about standing over the grill, tongs in hand, watching what the flames can do to the food.

if you can eat it, you can grill it, and there aren't many things you can't grill. Okay, well there are a few:

Eggs, for obvious reasons—though cracking one into a little foil cup and then cooking it on the grill is kinda cool.

Spaghetti—you could, but think of the hassle.

Cheese—mostly because of how it melts (but now that I've written that, see the Pastrami Grilled Grilled Cheese on page 96).

Food, grill, eat—it should be that straightforward. And that's what this book is about. Whether it's inside or outside, anyone with the most basic ingredients or equipment will be a star—and a well-fed one at that.

the equipment

This section in many grilling books occupies pages and pages and pages. Not here. It's not about the equipment; it's just about getting out there and doing something with it. For purposes of this book, I have used a gas grill. I suppose I am mostly a gas grill kinda guy. Not because I don't or can't appreciate the charcoal version—because I can. I just use a gas grill because I don't plan well in advance, and when I want to eat, I want to eat, and taking the requisite amount of time charcoal takes to do its thing is beyond me. Plus if I decide to halt things for a while I won't have to worry about adding more charcoal.

THE GRILL

That being said, I will suggest the rule of "use what you have." And if you have a big-ass place, get yourself a big-ass grill, because you'll likely invite over a big-ass crowd. If you have a small place, get a small grill, because you likely won't be having a ton of people over. Make sense?

Look, a $12,000 grill will cook a steak beautifully. So will a $25 hibachi, as long as you get it hot enough. And know this—everything you do outside, you can do inside. So even if you don't have a grill, no big deal—just read the section on indoor grilling (page 224), and buy the grill you can afford. Other than that, don't worry about it. The last thing I want is you sweating about not having a grill. Or worse, buying a stupidly expensive grill and getting annoyed every time you look at it because of the price.

THE TOOLS

Good tongs—that's it. And by good I mean "spring loaded." That '80s piece of bent metal your dad used in one hand (with a rum and Coke in his other) doesn't cut it. Oh, and those cases they sell full of BBQ tools for Father's Day are a mostly a waste of time and money. Spring-loaded tongs, not pokers, not grill forks, just tongs. I don't like forks because they poke holes in whatever's being cooked and the juices run out.

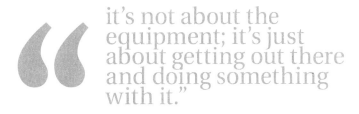

" it's not about the equipment; it's just about getting out there and doing something with it."

stuff to keep in your kitchen

A few things in your pantry or fridge can make your last-minute grill life much better. But not too many things, because one of the beautiful parts of grilling is that the grilling itself adds flavor.

IN THE SAUCE CATEGORY:

Hoisin Sauce—kind of like an Asian BBQ sauce. Can go on a lot of things (as you'll see) and adds a ton of flavor right from the jar.

Teriyaki Sauce—obvious, right?

BBQ—what, too obvious?

Canned Chipotles in Adobo—technically not a sauce, but add a little to the above BBQ sauce and you'll be styling with a little heat and only a little work.

Chili Sauce—this is related to the ketchup family, but with more flavor though not really spicy at all. You could easily use it anywhere that calls for ketchup.

Asian Chili Sauce—this is the really spicy version and a little goes a long way.

A Good Jarred Red & Green Salsa—you'd be surprised where these can help. And don't forget to read the section on how to fix something if you burn it up on the gril.

IN THE FROZEN FOOD CATEGORY:

Shrimp—for the most part, my food world is all about quick. Actually, make that quick and good—or "big in taste and small in effort" if this was an official Cooking Guy press thing. Shrimp, specifically frozen ones, are always a staple in my house. They defrost in no time and are great by themselves (page 178), in ceviche (page 185), or on top of a chimichurried steak (page 144).

Scallops—same deal as shrimp, and you'll be so glad you have them. Try them with the Mayo'd Steak Sauce (page 45).

Frozen Steaks—and before you get all up in my grill (so to speak) about these, you need to try them. My friend Joe has a terrible (read: "wonderful") habit of sending me steaks from a Chicago steak joint. They come frozen and have been some of the best steaks I've ever eaten—e-v-e-r. Don't make fun, because they're there when you want them, with no going out to the market.

IN THE GENERAL FOOD CATEGORY:

Olive Tapenade—you'll see I use it on a pizza (page 89) and on a fish thing (page 190). And even if you just use it on crackers, you'll be happy.

Really Good Extra Virgin Olive Oil—along with shrimp, I always mention this, and for good reason. Grilled food often doesn't require much more before serving than a nice drizzle of something luxurious, and this'll do it.

Kosher Salt & Fresh Ground Black Pepper—now, more than ever. Good seasoning is everything, and if this was all you had, you'd still kill it at the grill.

grilling do's & don'ts

A few simple rules to keep it all together for you—in no particular order. (Actually, that's not totally true; the order is how they came out of my head as I was writing.)

Take Meat Out Early—Take meat out of the fridge about 30 minutes before you plan on cooking it. You will not be eating meat that has gone bad, trust me. My wife does not believe that . . . she sees meat out of the fridge and puts it back. Then I take it back out, and she puts it back . . .

Don't do what she does. You can't possibly cook meat properly if it's fridge-cold in the middle.

Turn Your Grill to High 15 Minutes Before You Cook—Pretty much every time you grill, you leave some kind of residue on your grill that you need to burn off before you grill next time. I used to take my food off the grill and, leaving the burners on, close the lid to burn everything off. Unfortunately I'd forget, and go outside to my grill the next day and find a completely empty tank. I don't do that anymore. Now I remove the food and turn off the grill. Because you must heat your grill really well before you cook—so I use that time to burn off what was there from the time before. I finally got smart, and it only took 6 or so empty tanks to figure it out.

Keep Extra Gas Around—Even though you just read the paragraph above, and no matter how smart you might be, at some point you'll run out of gas—and it sucks when it happens. Having that emergency gas around will make it all better. Trust me—I know.

because you must heat your grill really well before you cook—i use that time to burn off what was there from the time before. **i finally got smart,** and it only took 6 or so empty tanks to figure it out."

Use More Heat—You'll see that most of the recipes in this book call for the heat at medium-high or high. More heat and less time is very often the key to success in grilling. Once the grill is hot, place your hand 3 inches above the grates. If you can hold it there for more than about 2 seconds, it's not hot enough.

Let a Steak Rest—When you pull a steak off the grill (or any meat for that matter), it needs time to let the juices reabsorb back into it. So cover it with foil and leave it for about 10 minutes. It will stay warm and be way juicier when you eventually get to it.

Times Are Approximate, Your Grill Ain't My Grill—Just because I say cook something for 10 minutes doesn't mean that will necessarily work perfectly for you. Remember the $12,000 grill vs. the $25 hibachi example? The hibachi will probably take longer, but will still be amazing. Just know that going in and be aware of it. And learn the Poke Test (page 133).

Get Yourself a Water Spray Bottle—We're talking about grilling on flames in this book. Stuff is going to catch on fire or flare up. There's no shame in keeping a water bottle at the ready just in case.

Sweet Sauces Will Burn if You Use Them Too Early—Things like the BBQ sauce I told you to keep in the house should only be applied in the last 5 minutes or so. They'll still add the flavor you want but won't burn and taste nasty.

Now that I've written all that, I realize it could be the most important page of the book. It's pretty simple stuff—but all important.

rubs & sauces

The grilling world can be a tough place—people tend to be a little, no make that a lot, protective about their sauces, etc. You hear things like, "My granddaddy made this sauce, and my daddy made this sauce and now me and the rest of the kin make this sauce." Okay, so maybe the "kin" part was a bit unnecessary, but you get the idea. When it comes to grilling, people like what they like. That being said, those people are probably not going to buy this book. Let's face it, a book with grilled meatballs, steak and mashed potato quesadillas, and a pastrami grilled cheese probably ain't for the kinfolk.

rubs

A rub is generally a combo of spices, herbs, and often some kind of sugar component that you simply rub onto the meat before cooking to give it flavor. The longer it's on the meat, the more flavor it'll give.

Just mix up the rub ingredients and then "rub" it into what it is you're cooking. Be generous with the rub and don't be shy with the rubbing, because the more rubbing, the more flavor you get.

A BASIC SEASONING RUB

¼ cup brown sugar

⅓ cup your favorite seasoning salt

Mix.
Use.

BASIC MEXICAN RUB

3 tablespoons chili powder

1 tablespoon cumin

1 tablespoon dried oregano

1 tablespoon garlic powder

1 teaspoon Kosher salt

Mix.
Use.

A SIMPLE PORK OR CHICKEN RUB

Chops, pork tenderloins, any chicken thing—it's all good. Lots of black pepper makes this one a fave . . .

- ¼ cup black pepper
- 2 tablespoons kosher salt
- 2 teaspoons cayenne pepper
- 2 teaspoons dry mustard
- 2 tablespoons paprika
- ¼ cup brown sugar

Mix.
Use.

SALT & PEPPER

Perhaps technically not a rub, but for me the simple mix of kosher salt and freshly ground black pepper is everything. You see, I like to taste whatever it's on—rather than a bunch of other things. So here is the easy little combo I keep already mixed. And when I cook a steak, this is all I use 98 percent of the time. Well, this and a little olive oil.

- ¼ cup kosher salt
- 2 tablespoons freshly ground
    black pepper

Mix.
Use.

wet rubs

Take a rub and add something moist and voilà, wet rub. It sticks more and therefore lets the flavors hang around more.

ROSEMARY & GARLIC RUB

This is my standard go-to when I grill a whole tenderloin.

- 1 tablespoon freshly ground black pepper
- 1 tablespoon kosher salt
- 3 tablespoons chopped fresh rosemary, or 1 tablespoon dried rosemary
- 5 cloves garlic, minced
- ⅓ cup olive oil

Put everything in a small bowl.
Stir gently to make a thick paste.
Use.

BASIC MEXICAN WET RUB

The wet here is the addition of the juice of 4 limes. Tangy and simply delicious. There are dry people and there are wet people—and this is for the latter, I guess.

- 3 tablespoons chili powder
- 1 tablespoon cumin
- 1 tablespoon dried oregano
- 1 tablespoon garlic powder
- 1 tablespoon Kosher salt
- ¼ cup fresh lime juice

Put everything in a small bowl.
Stir gently to make a thick paste.
Use.

"A sauce you can use for stuff on the grill offers huge potential for experimentation. I say you just **open the fridge and go for it**. Start mixing whatever you've got— a little sweet, a little sour, a little whatever. If you're not sure, be safe and simply try it out as a dip when the food comes off."

sauces

These generally go on the side or on top of something. You can make them and just have 'em in the fridge ready to use at a moment's notice.

ketchup

I like ketchup, but I don't like it plain, so I mix things in with it. Since you probably always have it on hand, you should almost always be able to make one of these.

pepper ketchup MAKES ABOUT ⅓ CUP

It may seem dopey, but this is maybe my favorite thing to dip fries into.
Try it once, at least.

⅓ cup ketchup
2 tablespoons coarsely ground black pepper

Mix.
Use.
Thank me.

pepper chili sauce MAKES ABOUT ½ CUP

Similar to the Pepper Ketchup. But I'm not calling for the super-hot Asian chili sauce in the ingredients list—I mean the kind of sauce that's sort of like ketchup, but with way more flavor.

⅓ cup chili sauce
2 tablespoons coarsely ground black pepper

Mix.
Use.
If you already thanked me for the ketchup version, we're good.
Go back to eating.

curry mayo MAKES ABOUT ½ CUP

Use this on fries, sandwiches, and veggies.

- ½ cup mayo
- 1 tablespoon curry powder
- 1 teaspoon regular mustard

Mix.
Use.

horseradish cream MAKES ABOUT 1 CUP

Amazing with beef.

- ¾ cup sour cream
- 2 tablespoons prepared horseradish
- 2 teaspoons olive oil
  Freshly ground black pepper

Mix all ingredients together.
Serve on the side with a steak.

"**Dogs were built for begging**, and Haley is no different. She can shoot you a look that would make you give up your last meal. We do our best not to give in, but with a face like that . . ."

truffle mayo MAKES ABOUT ½ CUP

Super good on a burger, fries, a BLT—a lot of stuff.

I'm the last guy to condone a crazy ingredient, but truffle oil isn't so crazy anymore. And since a little goes a long, long way, you can buy a tiny bottle for not much money. And whether you use it here, in the truffle ketchup below, or in scrambled eggs, mashed potatoes, or even popcorn—you'll dig it.

½ cup mayo
1 teaspoon white truffle oil
1 tablespoon chopped fresh parsley

Mix.
Use.

truffle ketchup MAKES ABOUT ½ CUP

½ cup ketchup
1 teaspoon white truffle oil

Mix.
Use.

peanut sauce MAKES ABOUT ½ CUP

¼ cup peanut butter (I prefer smooth here)

2 tablespoons soy sauce

2 tablespoons fresh lime juice

2 teaspoons chili paste

   Splash sesame oil

Mix all ingredients together in a small pot over low heat until combined.
Serve on the side with skewered grilled chicken or shrimp

peter's garlic sauce MAKES ABOUT ¾ CUP

In my first book I had a recipe for Jane's Motor Home Meatballs. Peter is Jane's son, and it only seemed right he got equal time. He's actually one of the most competent grill guys I know and will bust out the flames at the drop of a pin—or is it hat? Anyway, he says to use this as a marinade, grilling sauce, or super-condiment.

¼ cup ketchup
¼ cup vegetable oil
¼ cup soy sauce
4 cloves garlic, crushed

Mix all the ingredients together.
Use to grill, baste, marinate, or simply as a dipping sauce.

basil oil MAKES ABOUT 1¼ CUPS

1 cup fresh basil leaves
1 cup extra virgin olive oil
  Salt and freshly ground black pepper

Put the basil leaves and oil in a blender, season with salt and pepper, and whiz until smooth.

Put into a jar or squeeze bottle (I like a squeeze bottle).

Use it on everything and anything. It's perfect on fish or poultry before it hits the grill and veggies before, during, and after.

If you don't like the bits of basil—you can always strain them. But why bother?

garlic oil MAKES 1 CUP

Keeps in the fridge about a week and is so, so good on so, so many things.

1 **head garlic, cloves peeled**
1 **cup olive oil**

Put the garlic cloves and oil in a small pot—bring to a simmer.

Reduce the heat to low and cook until the garlic becomes light golden brown, about 15 minutes, but don't let it burn.

Let cool, strain the cloves from the oil, and put the oil into a squeeze bottle. Store in the fridge.

The grilling world is filled with ridiculous bravado, as in, "My stuff is better than your stuff." As in, "That ain't no sauce—this is a sauce." As in, "There seem to be more grilling and BBQ-ing competitions than with pretty much any other kind of cooking. And it's all about the trophies and bragging rights."

Why must it be like this? Why is everything a secret? Why can't you share your Uncle Billy-Bob's recipe for Tuscaloosa Chicken?

Why can't we all just get along? Why, why?"

mayo'd steak sauce MAKES ABOUT ¼ CUP

In addition to being very simple, this is also very good. So of course it would be great in a sandwich, but it really shines when you throw a couple tablespoons of it in at the last minute when stir-frying big shrimp. Or painted on some scallops shortly before they come off the grill. Whatever the application, you don't need a lot of it.

3 tablespoons mayo
1 tablespoon steak sauce

Combine, mix, use.

blue cheese mayo thing MAKES ABOUT A CUP

This works on a burger, as a dip for skewered chicken, grilled veggies, or even on a sandwich. I love it, but then, I love blue cheese on almost anything.

½ cup mayo
½ cup sour cream
2 ounces crumbled blue cheese
   Freshly ground black pepper, lots

Mix all the ingredients together.
Use—somehow, some way—soon.

mint yogurt sauce MAKE ABOUT A CUP

This goes stupidly well with anything lamb or veggie and is even great as an easy dip with the simply grilled pita on page 63.

1 cup plain yogurt, Greek-style if possible (it's thicker)
3 tablespoons chopped fresh mint
   Grated zest of 1 lime

Combine all the ingredients.
Use.

steak butters

A steak butter is just butter that's been mixed with some cheese, herbs, garlic, seasonings, or a combo of a bunch of them. And there's something beautifully wrong with taking a steak off the grill and topping it with a couple fat slices of a delicious butter.

The directions for the recipes below are the same, only the ingredients change.

Mix butter and other ingredients in a bowl with a spoon or spatula until well combined and very soft.

Put the butter in the middle of a piece of plastic wrap and roll into a log.

Twist the ends tightly to seal and put the tube of butter into the refrigerator to firm up.

The butters can stay in there about a week, or in the freezer about 2 months.

CHILI/LIME

1 stick butter, room temp
2 tablespoons chili powder
Juice of 1 small lime
2 teaspoons freshly ground black pepper

GREEN ONION GINGER

This one is especially good on fish.

1 stick butter, room temp
⅓ cup diced green onion (about 8 green onions)—white and light green parts only
1-inch piece fresh ginger, peeled and minced

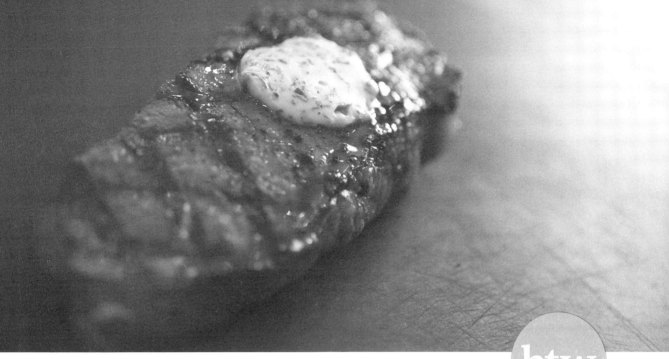

HERB-GARLIC

- 1 stick butter, room temp
- 3 small cloves garlic, minced
- 1 tablespoon olive oil
- ¼ cup chopped fresh herbs, whatever you've got—parsley, basil, oregano, chives, and rosemary all work great

MUSTARD

- 1 stick butter, room temp
- 3 tablespoons grainy mustard
- 1 teaspoon freshly ground black pepper

BLUE CHEESE

- 1 stick butter, room temp
- ⅓ cup crumbled blue cheese
- 2 tablespoons finely chopped chives or green onions

HORSERADISH BUTTER

- 1 stick butter, room temp
- 3 tablespoons prepared horseradish
- 3 tablespoons chopped Italian parsley

btw

Any of these steak butters could go just as deliciously well on a piece of grilled fish. So why not also call them "fish butters," you might wonder? Correct me if I'm wrong, but isn't there something pretty nasty-sounding about a "fish butter"?

small things.

tasty.

of my favorite things to do when entertaining is to have stuff already skewered and let my guests do the cooking. It gives them something to do and frees me up to do other things, or just lets me relax instead of cook. In fact, I prefer to leave as much of the appetizer section of the event to my guests as possible.

grilled shrimp cocktail MAKES ABOUT 60 SHRIMP

On big sporting-event weekends, New Year's Eve, and other occasions, supermarkets sell those ready-made shrimp cocktail party packs. You've seen them—the round, clear plastic containers with boiled pink shrimp lined up in a circle like the Radio City Rockettes at Christmas.

Well, they suck, so don't buy them.

- 1 cup chili sauce, not the Asian chili sauce—the ketchup kind
- 1 tablespoon prepared horseradish
- 1 teaspoon hot sauce (I use Cholula)
- ¼ teaspoon each kosher salt and freshly ground black pepper
- 1 lime, cut in half
- 60 shrimp (31/40s), peeled and deveined, but tails on
  Olive oil
- 10 wooden skewers, soaked in water about 30 minutes

Combine the chili sauce, horseradish, hot sauce, salt, pepper, and juice from 1 lime half—mix well and set aside.

Preheat the grill to medium-high.

Put 6 shrimp on each skewer, keeping them in their "c" shape.

Brush the shrimp lightly with olive oil and season with salt and pepper.

Grill the shrimp a couple minutes on each side until they are just done. Remove from the grill, squeeze on the remaining lime juice, and serve with the sauce.

grilled coconut shrimp MAKES ABOUT A DOZEN

Mmmm. I've got nothing else.

¾ cup coconut milk
    Juice of 1 lime
1 tablespoon soy sauce
1 to 2 tablespoons Asian chili sauce (see Sauce section)
2 teaspoons ground cumin
2 teaspoons curry powder
12 large shrimp (like U10s or 15s) peeled and deveined but with tails left on

Combine the coconut milk, lime juice, soy, chili sauce, cumin, and curry in a casserole dish. Add the shrimp, mix to coat the shrimp evenly, and refrigerate up to an hour.

Preheat the grill to medium-high.

Remove the shrimp from the coconut milk mix and place on the grill.

Cook until the shrimp are just done, maybe 3 to 4 minutes a side.

chicken with chipotle ranch MAKES 16 SKEWERS

Who doesn't always have ranch and chipotle around?
Wait—don't answer that.

16	small-ish bamboo skewers, 6 to 8 inches each (see BTW)
1	cup ranch dressing
1	to 2 canned chipotle peppers, minced
	Juice of 1 lime
8	chicken thighs
1	teaspoon chili powder
½	teaspoon each kosher salt and freshly ground black pepper
	Olive oil

Soak the skewers in water for about 30 minutes to help prevent them burning on the grill.

Combine the ranch, chipotle, and lime juice—I'd start with 1 chipotle; you can always add more if you want it spicier.

Cut each thigh into approximately 8 bite-sized pieces.

Combine the chili powder, salt, and pepper. Set aside.

Push 4 pieces of chicken onto each stick, and keep them near the top.

Lightly brush with olive oil, and season with the chili powder mix.

Preheat the grill to medium-high.

Grill the chicken until done, turning it to keep it from burning.

Serve with the ranch sauce.

I like to use small skewers and not put too much on each one. The idea is to skewer the food, not your tonsils, when you're eating.

buffalo wings MAKES ABOUT 30

These work well on skewers and I like to skewer each wing with 2 sticks—
you don't have to, but I find they just don't slip around as much.

60 wooden skewers
 1 cup Frank's Red Hot Sauce
½ cup (1 stick) butter
¼ cup brown sugar
 3 pounds chicken wings
   Blue Cheese Mayo Thing (page 46), for serving

Soak the skewers in water for about 30 minutes to help prevent them burning on the grill.

Meanwhile, combine the Frank's, butter, and brown sugar in a small pot (or
bowl in the microwave) and heat until melted—mix well. Set aside.

Preheat the grill to medium-high.

Skewer 2 wings on each stick. Place the wings on the grill and cook until
done on the first side, then flip.

Baste the now-cooked top side well a couple times during the bottom
cooking stage. When the bottom is done, flip them over and baste the
bottom well.

Remove to a plate, baste some more, and serve with the Blue Cheese
Mayo Thing.

the most basic (AND BEST) bruschetta ever

MAKES ABOUT 16 PIECES

There's not much better than a simply grilled baguette, some beautifully fresh tomatoes, a little garlic, and some basil. And good olive oil—don't forget that.

- 1 **pound ripe medium tomatoes**
- 1 **large clove garlic, a big boy**
- 1 **long French or sourdough baguette**
  Extra virgin olive oil
- ½ **cup loosely packed basil leaves, chopped pretty fine**
  Kosher salt and freshly ground black pepper

Preheat the grill to medium.

Cut the tomatoes into enough thick slices to cover the baguette.

Leaving the outer paper on the garlic, cut the clove in half. (The outer paper will keep your fingers from getting too garlicky.)

Slice the bread lengthwise, drizzle with oil, and grill face down until golden brown and crispy.

Remove the bread from the grill and immediately rub the cut side of the garlic clove all over the cut sides of the bread.

Layer the tomato slices on the cut side of the bread, then add the basil and sprinkle with salt and freshly ground black pepper.

Eat right away.

The key to this is amazingly ripe tomatoes. A ripe tomato should smell like a tomato, and have a little squish to it, but not too much. And more than any other tomato recipe, this is not the time for "maybe" ripe tomatoes. So if you're not sure what a nice ripe tomato is, ask your produce expert, cuz there's no shame in asking.

steak & mashed potato quesadillas

MAKES 2 QUESADILLAS

The wonderfulness of the Mashed Potato Taco from book #2 (*Awesome Recipes & Kitchen Shortcuts*) prompted me to revisit the age-old question "What more can I do with mashed potatoes?" This is it, and it makes sense for four good reasons:

- Because you're going to have leftover steak—you just are.
- Because where there's steak, there's probably potatoes.
- Because a grilled quesadilla is wonderful.
- Because why the hell not?

And who can argue with logic like that? So here it is—make it, eat it, love it.

> Olive oil
> 1 red onion, peeled and cut into ½-inch circles
> Kosher salt and freshly ground black pepper
> Four 8-inch flour tortillas
> 1 cup shredded smoked Gouda cheese
> 1 cup mashed potatoes, warmed
> 2 cups (about 10 ounces) leftover cooked steak, very thinly sliced

Preheat the grill to medium.

Lightly oil the onion slices, season with salt and pepper, and put on the grill.

Cook, turning once, until they soften and have good grill marks—remove to a bowl.

Turn the grill down to low.

Put 2 tortillas on 2 plates, sprinkle ¼ cup of the cheese on each, top each with half of the potatoes, add half of the steak to each, and finally add the remaining cheese to each. Top with the 2 remaining tortillas. Slide the quesadillas from the plates to the grill and grill until golden brown. Carefully flip the quesadillas over. Grill on the second side until the insides are warm and the tortillas are crispy.

Remove, cut into wedges, and serve.

jalapeño garlic bread MAKES 20 PIECES

Too good for words.

½ cup (1 stick) butter, softened
¾ cup grated Parmesan cheese
6 cloves garlic, peeled and minced, mashed, or squooshed
¼ cup diced jalapeños, and from a can is perfectly acceptable here
1 long loaf sourdough bread

Preheat the grill to medium (or turn on the broiler).

Mix together the butter, Parmesan, garlic, and jalapeños.

Slice the loaf lengthwise and spread the butter mixture on each cut side.

Place the bread, butter side down, on the grill and grill until golden brown.

Flip and cook on the other side for another minute or so.

Remove from the grill, cut into diagonal slices, and serve.

grilled cheesy pitas SERVES 4 TO 6

This is perfect with almost anything you take off the grill—plus they're much lighter than regular garlic bread (not that there's anything wrong with that). Try them alongside the Grilled Lamb Kebobs on page 163.

¼ cup grated Parmesan cheese
3 tablespoons olive oil (or Basil Oil if you have it, and you should if you read the beginning of the book, page 42)
2 cloves garlic, minced
   Four 6- to 8-inch pita breads

Preheat the grill to medium-high.

In a small bowl, combine the cheese, oil, and garlic. Mix well.

Brush both sides of the pita breads with the oil mixture and place on the grill. Grill for a couple minutes on each side or until golden.

Remove, cut into wedges, and serve.

fries

In a book that has a week's worth of burgers, and nearly as many hot dogs, there needed to be some discussion of fries. But if you know me even a little, you know I'm not making my own fries. More power to those who do, but I choose to skip anything that involves deep-frying. But that doesn't mean I don't do something with fries—because I do. And I like to serve them with different dips. Make sense? Just follow along and it will—and be sure to check out the Carne Asada Fries.

why

is grilling most often viewed as a man's job? Does it go back to caveman days? Is it because using fire outside is seen as more masculine? Or does the guy just want to get the hell out of the kitchen before he comes in contact with a salad or something?

Whatever the answer—it's now the twenty-first century and grilling should be everyone's domain. Everyone.

STEAK & MASHED POTATO QUESADILLAS (PAGE 60)

One of the things I've tried to encourage in this book is the idea that you don't have to eat something the same way you always do, and this is a perfect example. Frankly, it could be made with any leftover meat/poultry/seafood thing . . . but it just happens to be great with the steak.

SESAME GRILLED MEATBALLS (PAGE 80)

You hear foodies talk about "elevating" cuisine. This is not that. In fact, it might actually be the opposite of that sophisticated approach. I mean, think of it—meatballs on sticks on a grill. It's almost Neanderthal-like. And I love it.

CHEESY DOUGH BREAD (PAGE 90)

With all the fancy stuff you can put on a pizza, sometimes less is more. The fact that you're grilling pizza dough is almost good enough by itself. And the fact that it gets really really good with only a couple other things is the best.

STICKY SWEET RIBS (PAGE 169)

HONEY SOY LAMB CHOP (PAGE 165)

One of the easiest and most impressive things you can bust out is a grilled rack of lamb. Look how amazing it is, especially with the grill marks. I want it right now . . . .

MEXICAN GRILLED CORN (PAGE 123)

CHINESE GRILLED SHRIMP (PAGE 178)

Once you figure out how simple these are, you'll be grilling all kinds of different shrimp.
Unless my nephew Marc is coming over (like tonight), and then you won't be grilling any
kind of shrimp—he's a shrimp hater.

SNAPPER PUTTANESCA (PAGE 183)

PARMESAN HEARTS OF PALM (PAGE 116)

Look at them, just lying there waiting to be eaten. Drizzled with a little olive oil and then sprinkled with Parmesan cheese. So different, so delicious, so easy. Damn.

WHOLE GRILLED TROUT (PAGE 189)

The first time I did a whole trout was not too long ago, because I thought it would be a huge pain in the ass. Turns out, it's not even a little pain in the ass.

CRISPY GRILLED POLENTA (PAGE 115)

"SOMETHING" WITH OLIVE TAPENADE (PAGE 190)

EVERYDAY REALLY GOOD CLAMS & MUSSELS (PAGE 201)

In the dog days of summer, when you don't want to heat up the kitchen, you can still pull off this fantastic dish that's normally cooked in a pot on the stove. It's so darn good you should have it not in the dog days of summer—what?

THE DIRECTIONS ARE THE SAME, ONLY THE INGREDIENTS CHANGE:

1. Bake fries according to package directions.

2. Remove from oven and season right away with any of the combos below.

You'll wonder why you haven't been doing this for years.

SALT & PEPPER

Oh, you think this is too obvious? Well, if it is, why are you still reading?
You're reading because of the pepper. Salt would be obvious, but pepper . . .
no. Just do it.

ROSEMARY PARMESAN

Fresh rosemary if you happen to have it, but don't sweat it if you don't.
It's simply rosemary (chopped fine), Parmesan (I like the shredded rather
than the powder kind), and a bunch of kosher salt.

CHILI SALT FRIES

Equal parts chili powder and kosher salt.

CHINESE FIVE-SPICE

A simple little thing like this with some kosher salt makes everything
great. Once they're tossed, I like to dip them in Japanese mayo. I know I'm
mixing my cultures, but it works.

SEASONING SALT

Got nuthin' else? Just your everyday, garden-variety reddish seasoning salt
will totally perk up your fries.

carne asada fries SERVES ABOUT 4

A Southern California favorite . . . if you've never had them, you'll be glad you bought this book.

- 1 28-ounce bag frozen French fries
  About 1½ pounds leftover Carne Asada (page 143), chopped up small
- 2 cups shredded Colby/Jack cheese
- 1 cup guacamole
- ½ cup sour cream

Bake the fries according to the package directions.

Divide the fries among 4 plates. Top each one with some of the carne and then some of the cheese.

Microwave each plate for 30 to 60 seconds, or until cheese melts.

Remove and top with guacamole and then a little sour cream. Now that's what I'm talking about!

things not
normally
grilled.

impressive.

i like to cook things in ways you wouldn't normally think of cooking them. For example, in my first book, *Just a Bunch of Recipes* (nice plug, huh?), I suggest a grilled peanut butter and jelly. It's a wonderful thing because the insides get all warm and gooey and the outside gets crispy. It's with that thinking that I give you the stupidity, I mean, the brilliance of this chapter. Remember . . . pretty much anything you can cook inside, you can cook outside.

grilled baguette french toast
SERVES 4 (MAKES 8 PIECES EACH)

Anyone who has ever camped has likely made French toast on some kind of grill. And why not—it works. Not to mention it's pretty fun making breakfast for guests on your grill at home. Just don't forget sausages and bacon, which are also fantastic out there.

6 large eggs
½ cup milk
3 tablespoons maple syrup
1 French baguette
  Nonstick spray
  Powdered sugar

Preheat the grill to medium.

Beat the eggs well and stir in the milk and syrup.

Slice the bread lengthwise and then into 5-inch lengths.

Spray the grill with nonstick spray.

Dip both sides of the bread slices in the egg mixture, remove, and allow the excess to drip off and place on the grill (btw, this is a great time to try to get those grilled crosshatch marks on the bread—see page 132).

Cook until both sides are golden brown, remove, and serve with a fat sprinkle of powdered sugar.

grilled cheese

I know what you're thinking—you're thinking bread and cheese. But I don't mean that. I mean literally grilled "cheese." Haloumi is a Greek cheese that has a crazy high melting point and can therefore be panfried, broiled, or in our case grilled. I like to serve this on the side of a big salad with some great bread thing.

- **8 ounces haloumi cheese, in a block**
- **2 ounces (about ¼ cup) any oil-based salad dressing (I like Italian or Greek)**

Preheat the grill to medium.

Cut the cheese (that's funny) into ½-inch-thick slices, then brush with the dressing.

Grill until you get those cool grill marks, 2 to 3 minutes a side.

I like to cook salami on the grill. Just slice some into ⅛-inch rounds and make a few small cuts around the diameter to keep it from curling up too much. Get it a bit crispy, serve with a great mustard, and eat away. It's a fun appetizer to make while something else is taking much longer to cook.

mexican chicken on a mexican beer can

MAKES ONE 3- TO 4- POUND CHICKEN

I get a lot of e-mail, and one that regularly comes is from a guy—we'll call him "Nathan"—who watched me do beer can chicken on TV once. Nathan now writes to let me know every time he cooks one. It's always like, "Hey, Sam, remember me? I made it again last weekend and everyone loved it . . . " So when Nathan found out I was doing a grill book, I got an e-mail from him making sure I wouldn't forget to include the recipe. So here it is, just for Nathan, but you guys can read it too.

1 3- to 4-pound whole chicken (be sure to remove the bag of "stuff" from inside the bird)
⅓ cup Basic Mexican Wet Rub (page 31)
1 can Mexican beer, of course

Preheat the grill to high.

Rinse the chicken well and pat dry with paper towels. Rub the chicken with the wet rub inside and out.

Pour off or drink about half the beer and, being careful, push the chicken down onto the beer can so that the can goes into the umm, cavity. (Do I need to point out that the chicken has 2 cavities, and we're using the larger one?)

With the bottom of the can and the two legs making a sort of triangle support, I like to put the chicken and can on a small baking sheet first, then put that on the grill. Close the lid and cook the chicken over indirect heat (no flame directly under the chicken) for 1¼ to 1½ hours. If you're using a meat thermometer, you're looking for the chicken to be about 165°F in the breast area and 180°F in the thigh.

Let the chicken rest 10 minutes before you carve him. I mean "her." I mean "it."

grilled hearts of romaine SERVES 4

Yes, this is grilled, and it's just as much fun to make as it is to eat.

  2 hearts of romaine, basically a scaled-down version of the whole head
  ⅓ cup olive oil
     Balsamic vinegar
 16 slices cooked bacon, crumbled
  2 ripe medium tomatoes, diced
  ½ cup shredded Parmesan cheese
     Kosher salt and freshly ground black pepper
     Grilled Garlic Croutons (page 77)

Preheat the grill to medium.

Slice a thin piece ($\frac{1}{16}$ inch) off the core end of each romaine, just to clean it up. Then cut lengthwise down the middle of each romaine heart, making two equal halves.

Brush both sides of each half lightly with olive oil and place cut side down on the grill. Grill only a couple of minutes, just until the leaves begin to wilt. Flip and repeat.

Remove from the grill and place cut side up on the plate.

Sprinkle about a tablespoon of balsamic vinegar on each half, then drizzle with olive oil.

Add the bacon and tomatoes, and then top with cheese and season to taste with salt and pepper. Add the Grilled Garlic Croutons and serve.

grilled garlic croutons MAKES ABOUT 6 CUPS

These go perfectly with the grilled romaine salad.

1 sourdough baguette
Garlic Oil (page 43)

Preheat the grill to medium.

Slice the baguette lengthwise. Slice each half lengthwise into 3 long strips.

Drizzle each bread strip with the garlic oil.

Put the bread strips on the grill and watch them. Turn so all sides get some color, but not too much.

Remove from the grill and cut into cubes.

Now that you see how easily you can grill up some croutons, imagine all the other kinds you can make:

- Spread with a little butter and season with Creole seasoning, then grilled
- Drizzled with oil and hit with some BBQ rub or seasoning
- Drizzled with oil and sprinkled with a combo of chili powder and cumin for a little South of the Border flavor. Attention my Canadian family and friends: I mean Mexican flavor here, not American.
- Drizzled with oil and pounded with a ton of chopped-up fresh herbs

You get where I'm going with this, right? You're only limited by your imagination . . .

meatloaf on the grill SERVES 6 TO 8

I put this in the same category as a hot dog. Most of us are not making our own hot dogs, right? And even though there's a super delicious recipe for a Mexican Meatloaf in my last book, *Awesome Recipes & Kitchen Shortcuts,* I realize sometimes you might just pick up a meatloaf from the store already made. Wanna call it cheating? Fine. I call it being smart and eating well.

- 1 cup American chili sauce
- ½ cup brown sugar
- 2 tablespoons Worcestershire sauce
- 1 store-bought, already-cooked meatloaf

Preheat the grill to medium.

Mix together the chili sauce, brown sugar, and Worcestershire sauce.

Cut the meatloaf into 1½-inch-thick slices.

Brush the glaze on the meatloaf slices and grill until heated through and nicely browned.

Serve.

This is so easy that when you're invited to bring something to a backyard BBQ, take this along.

sesame grilled meatballs MAKES 32 MEATBALLS

So I'm sitting here one day working on this book and I think to myself, why couldn't you do meatballs on a grill? And guess what—turns out you can, and they're way easy, way fun, and way good. Who knew?

About ½ cup hoisin sauce

1 teaspoon Asian chili sauce

32 small meatballs, about a pound (the fully cooked frozen kind), defrosted

¼ cup sesame oil

32 small bamboo skewers, approximately 6 inches

¼ cup finely chopped green onions

Preheat the grill to medium-high.

Mix the hoisin and chili sauce together; set aside.

Brush the meatballs with the oil, scatter them on the grill and cook until fully warmed through and starting to brown, with grill markings.

Remove the meatballs from the grill and skewer each. Put on serving plates, top with some green onions, and serve with the hoisin mix for dipping.

I like to use frozen small meatballs. They're about ½ ounce each. If you make the "Okay" sign with your thumb and forefinger, they're about the size that would fit in that circle. And they are perfect for appetizers, sandwiches, or whatever else you can come up with.

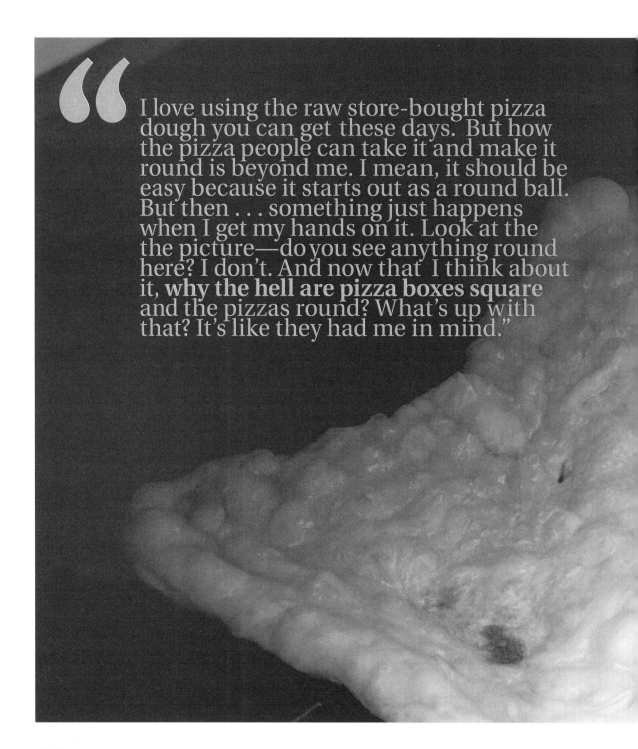

"I love using the raw store-bought pizza dough you can get these days. But how the pizza people can take it and make it round is beyond me. I mean, it should be easy because it starts out as a round ball. But then . . . something just happens when I get my hands on it. Look at the the picture—do you see anything round here? I don't. And now that I think about it, **why the hell are pizza boxes square** and the pizzas round? What's up with that? It's like they had me in mind."

pizza

Pizza on a grill is a glorious thing. Making the dough is not—or at least for me it isn't. So I have no intention on giving you a recipe for pizza dough. I buy raw dough already made from a store or get it from a pizza place. The smaller pizza restaurants are usually happy to sell you dough for you to deal with.

THE KEY TO COOKING A PIZZA USING RAW DOUGH IS SIMPLE:

1. Remove the dough from the fridge about 30 minutes before using.

2. Spread some flour on a work surface in an area larger than your pizza will be.

3. Gently stretch out the dough into a circle until it's about ¼ inch thick—I say circle, but more often than not mine end up in some weird and bizarrely unrecognizable shape.

4. Brush the top lightly with oil and put it oil side down on a medium-hot grill.

5. Once the bottom has browned with those great grill marks, oil the top and flip it over.

6. Turn the grill down (or move the pizza to a less hot part of the grill), brush the no browned top with oil once again, and put on whatever topping you plan to use. Close the lid.

7. Now just wait for the magic—you're probably only 5 to 7 minutes from being done.

And now that you know what to do, you can make one of these:

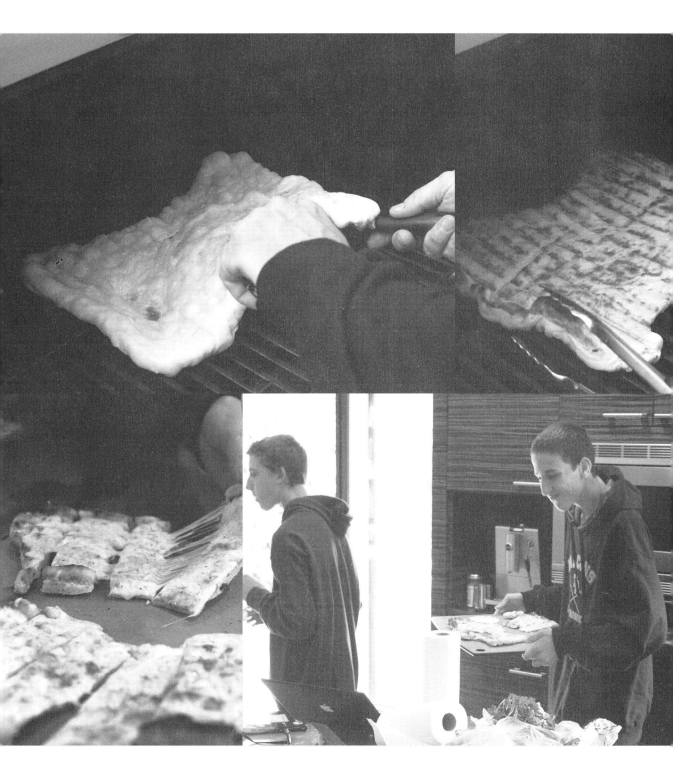

grilled veggie MAKES 1 PIZZA

This is the reason to have leftover vegetables.

>   About 2 cups mixed grilled veggies (see recipe on page 110)
>   Dough for about a 10- to 12-inch pizza
>   Basil Oil (page 42)
> 4 ounces feta cheese, crumbled

Prepare the veggies by cutting into sort-of-thin strips—this just makes the eating more manageable.

Follow the directions on page 84 for grilling pizza, and when you get to step 6, top with the sliced veggies, drizzle with the Basil Oil, and then crumble the feta over the top.

Move to a less hot part of the grill and continue cooking until done.

Slice and serve.

caramelized onion & bacon MAKES 1 PIZZA

Sweet red onions, bacon, and blue cheese—how do you spell "home run"? I know I just spelled it—it's just an expression.

   Olive oil
1 **large red onion, sliced thin**
1 **tablespoon brown sugar**
   Enough uncooked dough for 1 pizza
2 **ounces "ready bacon," cut into ½-inch pieces and cooked until almost crispy**
4 **ounces blue cheese, crumbled**
½ **cup shredded mozzarella**

In a nonstick pan, heat a tablespoon of oil over medium heat and cook the onions, stirring, until they begin to get very soft, about 10 minutes. Add the brown sugar, mix well, and set aside.

Follow the directions on page 84 for grilling pizza, and when you get to step 6, brush the marked top with olive oil, then add the onions, bacon, blue cheese, and mozzarella.

Move to a less hot part of the grill and continue cooking until done.

Slice and serve.

A fun thing to do is to dip the doughy bread into a warm, thick tomato kinda sauce, a ranch-like dip, or anything fun.

grilled bacon & mashed potato
MAKES 1 PIZZA

An amazingly stupid-sounding but fantastic combo. And I figured since we were on the topic of bacon . . . works well with a store-bought crust (see BTW if you do).

2	tablespoons garlic oil (page 43)
1	ball pizza dough
1½	cups cooked mashed potatoes
1	large clove garlic, minced
2	ounces "ready bacon," diced and cooked until crispy
½	cup shredded Monterey Jack cheese

Lightly oil a baking sheet and spread the dough until it's about ¼ to ⅓ inch thick. It doesn't need to be a perfect circle (in fact, it rarely is).

Warm the potatoes in a small pot on the stove.

Heat the grill to medium.

Follow the directions on page 84 for grilling pizza, and when you get to step 6, brush the top with the garlic oil, then spread with the mashed potatoes and bacon, and sprinkle with the cheese.

Close the grill lid and let cook until the cheese melts, about 3 or 4 more minutes.

Remove, slice, and eat—but that was obvious, right?

For a store-bought ready crust, brush the top with garlic oil, then add the potatoes, bacon, and cheese and bake in a 425°F oven for about 12 minutes.

spicy olive tapenade & prosciutto

MAKES 1 PIZZA

If you missed the tapenade part in the "what to keep on hand" section (page 21), go read it now. And if you read it, way to go!

½ cup store-bought olive tapenade
1 teaspoon red pepper flakes
Enough uncooked dough for 1 pizza
Olive oil
4 ounces sliced prosciutto
1 cup shredded mozzarella

Mix together the tapenade and pepper flakes.

Follow the directions on page 84 for grilling pizza, and when you get to step 6, spread the tapenade on the crust, then cover with the prosciutto and mozzarella

Move to a less hot part of the grill and continue cooking until done.

Slice and serve.

cheesy dough bread SERVES ABOUT 6

You're basically making a very simple cheese pizza, but one with no sauce and that's way more sensual 'cuz it's soft and doughier.

Enough uncooked dough for one pizza
1 **cup of your favorite cheese (you could go with a simple shredded mozzarella and that would be fine, but what about a smoked Gouda or a pepper jack or a horseradish cheddar? See where I'm going here?)**
Olive oil

Follow the directions on page 84 for gilling pizza. When you get to step 6, lightly brush the top with olive oil and add the cheese of your choice and any herbs you might be using.

Close the lid and let the cheese melt, but be careful to keep the whole thing from getting too crispy.

Remove, pull off a chunk or two, and eat.

A fun thing to do is to dip the doughy bread into a warm, thick tomato kinda sauce, a ranch-like dip, or anything fun.

When asked to bring something to a backyard BBQ, you have many options. Sadly, though, many people default to a salad. I mean—a salad is okay, but a little boring. I like taking things people don't expect and even cooking them there. Of course Kelly and I always argue about this—she says it's not right to go to someone's place and start using their grill, oven, stove—whatever. I say if they ask me to bring something, they need to deal with whatever I bring. And things like the Grilled Meatballs or Steak & Mashed Potato Quesadilla are perfect.

And trust me: No one will complain if the food you bring is good."

my favorite cooking guy sandwiches.

savory.

grill is often overlooked at lunch, and that's kinda sad. That being said, anytime is the right time for a sandwich. So I say bust these out at night, morning, or whenever.

pastrami grilled grilled cheese
MAKES 1 REAL, TOTALLY LEGIT *GRILLED* CHEESE

We all call it a "grilled cheese sandwich," but how often is it really grilled, as in a BBQ grill? I'd say almost never, unless you were over here for lunch a few days ago. The rules all mostly stay the same—it's just the cooking venue that changes.

2 tablespoons butter, softened

1 clove garlic, minced, crushed, or chopped fine

2 slices sourdough bread

1 tablespoon horseradish sauce—the mayo kind, not the grainy "prepared" kind

2 slices cheddar cheese

   Enough thinly sliced pastrami to cover one piece of the bread—don't skimp—and heated lightly on the grill first

2 slices jack, Muenster, provolone, or whatever

Preheat the grill to medium-low.

Put the butter and garlic in a small bowl and mix well.

On one slice of bread, spread the horseradish sauce. Add the 2 slices of cheddar cheese, then the warmed pastrami, the other slices of cheese, and then top with the last slice of bread.

Spread half the butter/garlic mixture on the outside of one side of the sandwich and cook on the grill, buttered side down, until golden brown with those cool grill marks.

Butter the top side, flip, and continue grilling until the bottom is golden as well.

Eat—but not too quickly, even though you'll want to.

"I get asked often why, when I'm shooting a show, do I eat really hot food and burn my mouth. The answer is simple—because **I do the same thing** when I'm totally alone and there are no cameras around. It may not be the brightest move, but it's what I do. And I try to be the same on-camera as off."

chicken parmesan sub MAKES ONE 4-PERSON SUB

Not like grandma made—no heavy breading or thick sauce. Just simple grilled chicken with grilled tomatoes taking the place of the sauce.

- 5 to 6 boneless chicken thighs, trimmed of unnecessary fat
- 3 to 4 tablespoons olive oil, plus extra for drizzling
- 1 tablespoon dried oregano
  Kosher salt and freshly ground black pepper to taste
- 2 medium-sized ripe tomatoes
  One of those short ciabatta-type baguettes
- ½ cup shredded mozzarella cheese
  About ½ cup fresh basil leaves, or enough to cover one side of the bread

Put the chicken in a zipper-top plastic bag, add the olive oil and oregano, and season well with salt and pepper. Mix well. Refrigerate about 30 minutes .

Preheat the grill.

Thickly slice the tomatoes and drizzle with olive oil on both sides.

Cut the bread in half lengthwise and drizzle both sides with olive oil.

Grill the chicken on the first side until beautifully done, about 5 minutes. Turn the chicken over, then put the tomatoes on the grill and grill both sides until they get soft.

Place the bread on the grill and toast it.

Sprinkle the shredded mozzarella on the chicken to melt while everything finishes.

Build your sandwich like this: bottom of bread, chicken, tomato, basil, and top of bread. Slice into 4 equal pieces and eat.

bbq shrimp po' boy

SERVES 3—MAYBE 4, BUT PROBABLY 3. YEAH, 3 SEEMS RIGHT.

A classic New Orleans–type of sandwich. But instead of a pain-in-the-ass deep-fried concoction, it's done on the grill. Who's the "King of Easy" now? Huh? Huh?

SAUCE

- ¼ cup mayo
- ¼ cup finely diced red onion
- 2 tablespoons American chili sauce
- 1 tablespoon prepared horseradish
- 2 teaspoons hot sauce

SHRIMP PO' BOY

- ¾ pound raw shrimp (21/25s), shell off and deveined
- ½ teaspoon cayenne
- Olive oil
- Kosher salt and freshly ground black pepper
- 4 French rolls, the sandwich type/ size
- Shredded iceberg lettuce, about a cup
- Sliced tomatoes

Preheat the grill to medium.

To make the sauce, combine the mayo, onion, chili sauce, horseradish, and hot sauce. Mix well and set aside.

Mix the shrimp with the cayenne and 1 tablespoon of olive oil and season with salt and pepper.

Grill the shrimp on both sides until just done—juicy and amazing, not dried out and disgusting.

Slice the rolls lengthwise, drizzle with olive oil on the cut side, place cut side down on the grill, and grill slightly.

Build po' boys with the shrimp, sauce, lettuce, and tomatoes.

Eat quickly and then make another one . . .

on the grill ribeye philly PROBABLY MAKES 4 SANDWICHES

Here's the thing—I've never been to Philadelphia, I don't know anyone from there, and even if I did, I'm sure they would say you can't make this on a grill. But you know what? I don't worry about them because this is awesome without their advice.

Just make it and enjoy it.

Olive oil
1 **pound ribeye steak**
Kosher salt and freshly ground black pepper
1 **green bell pepper, the 4 sides cut off (discard the core)**
1 **yellow onion, cut into ½-inch-thick round slices**
2 **tablespoons Worcestershire sauce**
4 **fresh sandwich rolls, split in half crosswise and lightly grilled**
4 **slices provolone cheese**

Preheat the grill to medium-high.

Lightly oil the steak, then season it with salt and pepper.

Place the steak on the grill and cook until medium rare, about 5 minutes per side. Remove and cover with foil. Keep warm.

Drizzle the pepper and onion slices with olive oil, put on the grill, and cook until all are soft and really well marked. Remove from the grill, chop roughly into thin slices, put in a bowl, and add the Worcestershire and some salt and pepper.

Mix.

Thinly slice the steak across the grain, put some on a roll, add the pepper/onion mixture, then top with cheese and the top of the roll.

grilled cuban MAKES 4 SANDWICHES

Cuban sandwiches are really popular in Florida, as in really popular. And though they're normally grilled in a sandwich press, we're going to use the grill. You'll just need to find a heavy object to weight it down. A cast-iron pan would be ideal.

- 4 good Italian or French rolls
- ¼ cup yellow mustard
- ⅓ pound deli ham, thinly sliced
- ⅓ pound cooked pork tenderloin, thinly sliced (use the pork in the Pork "Jerked" Tacos, page 158)
- 4 dill pickles, in thin slices
- ⅓ pound Swiss cheese, thinly sliced
- ¼ cup butter

Preheat the grill to medium.

Slice each roll, leaving a hinge. Spread the mustard on one side and then add the ham, pork, pickles, and Swiss cheese.

Close up the sandwich and press down to flatten a little. Spread one side with butter.

Put the sandwiches, butter side down, on the grill and put something heavy on top to flatten. Grill the sandwiches until golden brown, butter the top, flip, put the heavy thing back on top, and continue until both sides are beautiful and the cheese has melted.

Remove from the grill, cut in half, and serve.

Enjoy, mi buen amigo.

vegetables.

delish.

crazy thing about veggies is they are one of the few things that can be really great with almost nothing being done to them— but show them a little grilling love and look the hell out, BOOM . . . magic happens.

grill these veggies and you'll be a star

SERVES 8 TO 10

Not only can nearly all veggies be grilled, but they should be, because it might just be the best way to cook them. Make the Grilled Veggie Pizza on page 86 with the leftovers.

2	red bell peppers
2	yellow bell peppers
2	red onions
2	globe eggplants
4	small yellow squash
4	small zucchini

2	pounds asparagus
2	pounds cherry tomatoes
$\frac{1}{3}$	cup basil oil (see BTW)
	Kosher salt and freshly ground black pepper

Preheat the grill to medium-high.

Cut the sides off the peppers—remove the ribs, core, and any seeds.

Peel the outside paper from the onions, cut off the ends, and slice into ½-inch-thick rounds.

Remove the ends from the eggplants, then cut into ½-inch thick rounds.

Remove the ends from the squash and zucchini, then cut lengthwise into ½-inch-thick slices.

Cut about ½ inch from the tough ends of the asparagus (or is it asparagi?).

Place all the veggies on a baking sheet, brush all sides lightly with basil oil, and season with salt and pepper.

Grill (see BTW) until marks appear, turning as necessary. Brush with the basil oil again as they come off the grill.

Serve with pretty much anything.

Grill the veggies in the order they are on the ingredient list. The peppers will take the longest and the tomatoes the least. You're trying to keep them crisp/tender—not mushy, but not too hard either.

If you can't find basil oil in the store, follow the recipe in the sauces section (page 42) to make your own.

wasabi mashed potatoes MAKES ABOUT 2 CUPS

Okay, so obviously this is not something you can do on a grill, but it goes
so well with a lot of the stuff you can, it seemed a shame not to include it.

2 cups mashed potatoes (I use store-bought—if you want a recipe for
   mashed potatoes from scratch, buy another book)
2 tablespoons sour cream
1 to 2 tablespoons wasabi paste
   Kosher salt and freshly ground black pepper to taste

Mix everything (meaning as much wasabi as you can take) together and
keep warm until serving.

I can't remember the last time I ate plain
mashed potatoes. I mean, I almost always
put something in them, and the list is
endless: cheese, bacon, hot sauce, herbs,
pesto, sour cream, ranch dressing, hot
peppers—**it doesn't matter**. You can pretty
much find something to add that'll match
the rest of your meal. It just makes it way
more fun."

crispy grilled polenta SERVES 6

This is a hugely overlooked premade item in the supermarket. Polenta is made with cornmeal and most often served in restaurants as a creamy, porridge kind of thing—which sounds bad and reminds me of *Oliver!*, as in, "Please sir, can I have some more . . . ?" But that's not the one I'm talking about. This one has already been formed into the shape of a giant sausage, sort of, which, funny enough, also sounds bad. But it's not—you just cut a few rounds off of it, drizzle with oil, add some seasonings and herbs, and grill. It's wonderful; just do it.

1 **tube prepared polenta**
Basil Oil (page 42)
Kosher salt and freshly ground black pepper

Preheat the grill to medium-high.

Cut the polenta into ¾-inch-thick rounds. Brush with the oil and season with salt and pepper.

Grill the polenta rounds on both sides until nicely marked, about 7 to 10 minutes a side—and don't move them while they cook or you'll jack with the cooking process and they'll stick and bust.

Remove and serve sorta like a side of potato something.

And once you get this whole polenta thing down, try some of these ideas.

Remove from the grill and:

Spoon on a little warm pesto and Parmesan cheese on top.

Serve with the grilled veggies from page 110.

Sauté some mushrooms and serve them on top of the polenta with an extra drizzle of really good olive oil.

parmesan hearts of palm SERVES 6 TO 8

A heart of palm is the white tube-shaped sort of asparagus-tasting thing that comes from the inner core of certain palm trees. It's most often used cold in salads. We're going to grill it, and it's going to kick ass. Serve it on the side like you would grilled asparagus.

2 **14-ounce cans hearts of palm, drained, rinsed, and patted dry**
    2 to 3 tablespoons olive oil
    Kosher salt and freshly ground black pepper to taste
    Balsamic vinegar
3 **tablespoons shredded Parmesan cheese**

Preheat the grill to medium-high.

Drizzle the hearts lightly with oil, then season with salt and pepper.

Put the hearts on the grill and cook they're until nicely marked all around, about 15 minutes total.

Remove from the grill, transfer to plates, and while the hearts are still warm, drizzle lightly with the vinegar and sprinkle with the cheese and a little more pepper.

Serve.

grilled pineapple salsa MAKES ABOUT 3 CUPS

Perfect with any fish or chicken thing—like a skewered one.

- 1 pineapple, rind removed, cored, and cut into ½-inch-thick slices
- 2 tablespoons butter, melted
- ½ cup red onion, diced small
- ¼ cup chopped fresh cilantro
- 2 tablespoons fresh lime juice
- 1 teaspoon peeled and minced fresh ginger
- ½ teaspoon grated lime zest
- ⅛ teaspoon cayenne pepper
- Kosher salt and freshly ground black pepper

Preheat the grill to medium-high.

Brush the pineapple slices with the butter and place the slices on the grill.

Grill the pineapple slices until lightly charred on both sides.

Remove from the grill, chop into small dice, and put into a bowl.

Add the onion, cilantro, lime juice, ginger, lime zest, and cayenne to the bowl and season with salt and pepper.

Let stand about 20 minutes. If you make it in advance, cover and refrigerate the salsa, but bring to room temp before serving.

pommes de terre dans un sac (POTATOES IN A BAG)

SERVES 4

There was absolutely no reason for me to put that title up there in French. Plus it's probably not even an accurate translation. (It's been years since my French class with Mrs. Arthurs.) But potatoes can be a little difficult to do on the grill, so we put them in a foil bag, add a few things, and they cook beautifully. Plus it's like opening a present when they're ready, and who doesn't like a present?

- 2 pounds small red potatoes, washed and thinly sliced
- 1 small red onion, thinly sliced
- 1 red pepper, thinly sliced
- 1 clove garlic, minced (you thought I was going to say "thinly sliced" didn't you?)
- 2 teaspoons minced rosemary, thyme, oregano, or any herb you dig, preferably fresh—even a combo of them all
- 2 to 3 tablespoons olive oil
  Kosher salt and freshly ground black pepper
  Aluminum foil

Preheat the grill to medium-high.

Mix everything in a large bowl (except the foil, cuz that would suck, right?).

Tear off 4 sheets of foil, each about 2 feet long, fold over, and put ¼ of the potatoes in the middle of each.

Fold the sides in to make a little packet, being sure to seal the sides well—you want to keep the steam in.

Grill for about 30 minutes, and flip about halfway through. They are done when, well, they are done. You'd know when a potato was done, wouldn't you?

sautéed mushrooms MAKES 4 SERVINGS

Perfect with any fish or chicken thing—like a skewered one.

- 2 tablespoons butter
- ½ tablespoon olive oil
- 1 garlic clove, minced
- 1 pound sliced mushrooms, any kind
  Kosher salt and freshly ground black pepper
- ¼ cup white wine or vermouth

Put the butter and oil in a large skillet over medium heat. When it starts to melt, add the garlic and then the mushrooms and cook slowly, stirring occasionally, until tender, about 15 minutes.

Season well with salt and pepper.

Move the pan away from the heat and add the wine.

Allow the alcohol to burn off a little, then put back on the stove.

Mix well and serve.

HERB MUSHROOMS—Same as above, but add bunch of fresh herbs after the wine—like parsley, thyme, rosemary, etc.

RED WINE MUSHROOMS—Same as above, but substitute red wine for the white wine.

SOY MUSHROOMS—Same as above, but substitute soy sauce for the wine.

TERIYAKI MUSHROOMS—Same as above, but substitute teriyaki sauce for the wine.

cucumber & watermelon salad SERVES 4

This is refreshing, delicious and pretty, so what more do you need? You want it simple? Okay then, simple too. The key is to cut everything into cubes somewhere around 1-inch square.

- 2 cups peeled and cubed cucumber (an English cucumber is best)
- 2 cups cubed seedless watermelon
- 2 avocados, peeled, seeded and cubed
- 3 tablespoons extra virgin olive oil
- 2 tablespoons balsamic vinegar
- 1 tablespoon each chopped cilantro, basil and chives
     Kosher salt and freshly ground black pepper

Put the cucumber, watermelon, avocado, olive oil, vinegar, and herbs in a large bowl. Season with salt and pepper.

Mix well, but do it carefully so you do not bust up the watermelon.

Serve.

mexican grilled corn

MAKES 6 EARS—THAT SOUNDS SILLY, DOESN'T IT?

Have it once, and you'll have it forever—unless of course you're my wife, and then you'll have it never. Have I mentioned she's my food opposite?

- 6 chopsticks, not pairs, just 6 sticks
- 6 ears of corns, husks and the crazy pain-in-the-ass silk removed
- ½ cup mayonnaise
- ⅓ cup grated Parmesan cheese
- 2 tablespoons chili powder
- 6 lime wedges

Preheat the grill to medium.

With a small knife, make an X about ¼ inch deep in the middle of the bottom of each ear; this is where the handle will go.

Give the corn a quick rinse under cold water and place directly on the grill.

Place on the grill and cook until softened and golden brown in spots, up to about 30 minutes.

Remove from the grill and push the chopstick into the X you made in each ear, making a handle. Using the back of a spoon or a pastry brush, brush each ear with the mayo—and don't be shy.

Sprinkle with the Parmesan and then a little dusting of chili powder. Give 'em a quick squeeze of lime and away you go—corn nirvana.

If you're jacked for time, you can always wrap the ears in plastic wrap and give them a zap in the microwave for about 3 minutes, then throw them on the grill. It'll cut the cooking time waaaay down.

the best cauliflower SERVES 6

I pushed cauliflower off my plate until about a year ago. I felt it was just a useless vegetable. But now that I've grilled it, it's a whole new world. Broccoli is still useless, but not cauliflower anymore.

⅓ cup olive oil

2 cloves garlic, mashed

½ teaspoon kosher salt

1 teaspoon cayenne pepper

1 teaspoon freshly ground black pepper

1 head cauliflower

Preheat the grill to medium.

Mix together the oil, garlic, salt, cayenne, and pepper.

Cut the cauliflower into quarters, being careful to keep the stem attached so it doesn't fall apart.

Brush all over with the oil mix.

Grill for about 5 to 10 minutes a side, or until it gets kinda crispy but soft enough to eat. Remove from the grill and brush once more before serving.

a really great no mayo potato salad
SERVES 8

Any grilling book needs a potato salad—and here's mine. But I don't use mayo in this—not because I don't want the mayo, I just don't want the mayo fat (and I don't like fat-free mayo). And who needs mayo when a potato salad tastes this good?

1	tablespoon salt
2	pounds small white or red (or both) potatoes
$\frac{1}{2}$	cup diced celery
$\frac{1}{3}$	cup diced green onion
$\frac{1}{2}$	cup small diced red onion
$\frac{1}{4}$	cup chopped fresh parsley
5	hard-boiled large eggs, peeled and sliced
12	pieces cooked bacon, crispy and diced up
$\frac{1}{3}$	cup honey Dijon dressing
	Kosher salt and freshly ground black pepper to taste

Bring a large pot of water to a boil, add the salt, and then the potatoes.

Cook until the potatoes are tender enough to poke a knife through easily, about 15 minutes, then drain and allow to cool for about 10 minutes.

When the potatoes are cool enough to handle (but still a little warm), cut them into quarters and put in a large bowl. Add the celery, onions, parsley, eggs, bacon, and dressing. Season well with salt and pepper, then mix well.

Serve cold or at room temperature.

This is something you can easily make early in the day or even the day before; be sure to give it a fresh sprinkling of chopped parsley if you do.

mmm.

yes, for many beef is the holy grail of grilling. But should it be? I just mean I know plenty of people who don't even eat the stuff—so why all the fuss? And for all the noise, I believe there's more beef being ruined on grills around the world than almost anything else. And that's a shame, but I think I know why.

I talk food with a lot of people and I always ask if they cook and what they cook. About 65 percent of the time, the women take responsibility for most of the cooking, but go on to say that their men (if they do anything) do the grilling.

Well, you know how men hate asking for directions? It's the same here. The guy mutters a quick "I've got it, hon," and he heads out to grill because he is the man after all, and that's what men do. And then he proceeds to burn the #@*% out of whatever it is he has.

So let me help the situation right now—it takes practice. Let's use my favorite bike analogy. Remember the first time you rode? You probably fell off, but you got better each time after that, right? Well, grilling beef, more than anything else, takes practice. So here are four very important words you need to hear (or read—this is a book after all):

BUY AN EXTRA STEAK!

Let's say you have company over and you need to grill 4 steaks. The last thing you want to do is cut into one of the steaks you're going to serve, because it just looks messy, and it lets all the juices out and that's bad. So rather than take a chance with your guest's main course, you could throw an extra steak on the grill and use it to determine how the rest are doing. And it won't be a waste, because there are a ton of things you can make with a leftover steak (see what to Do With Leftover Steak on page 147).

I'd love for you to get to the point where you judge a steak's doneness by touch—and guess how you can get there? By touching, (see Poke Test below) and by having an extra steak around to practice on first. So the next time you see some New York ribeyes or sirloins on sale, buy a couple. And get out to the grill. And pay attention to these important tips:

- Get your steak out of the fridge 20 to 30 minutes before cooking.

- Heat your grill really well—crank it to high at least 15 minutes before cooking.

- Brush the steak lightly with olive oil, and season well with kosher salt and freshly ground black pepper.

- Put it on the grill and leave it. Don't stab it, don't prod it—don't do any thing.

- Plan to cook it no more than about 5 minutes on the first side for a steak about an inch and a half thick.

- If you want those crosshatch marks (I don't, but you might), start the steak on a diagonal to the grates, and then turn it 90 degrees after 3 minutes. Leave it for another couple minutes, then flip and do the same on the back, but for only a couple minutes each turn.

In general, the second side will likely take about a minute less time.

- Remove the steak from the grill, cover it with foil, and let it sit for about 10 minutes before eating. To know if it's done, you have a few choices:

  ✳ Cut into it while it cooks—bad idea.

  ✳ Use an instant-read thermometer. Okay idea, but what's the right temp? A quick check of neighbors, friends, and even experts will turn up a wide range of temperatures. For example, you can find suggested temps for medium rare ranging from 125°F all the way to 145°F. That's a big difference. I prefer around 130°F.

  ✳ Learn to test by touch—now you're talking.

Try learning the Poke Test:

  ✳ Keeping your hand loose, make a circle with your thumb and forefinger, then push on the fat pad under your thumb. This is what rare should feel like when you push down on the cooked steak.

  ✳ Now use your thumb and middle finger—this is what medium rare should feel like.

  ✳ Finally, use your thumb and ring finger and, you guessed it—well done. But personally, I think no steak should ever be well done. You just lose so much flavor that way.

The key really is to just get out there and throw something on the grill and start. You can't get better if you don't start.

my favorite way to eat steak MAKES ENOUGH FOR ME

I would rather eat a good piece of meat less often than eat a crappy piece of meat all the time. So I prefer a filet, simply prepared. I always look for them on sale (see BTW).

1 **6- to 8-ounce filet mignon**
Extra virgin olive oil
Kosher salt and freshly ground black pepper
Blue cheese crumbles

Remove the filet from the fridge 30 minutes before cooking.

Preheat the grill to high.

Brush lightly with olive oil, then season well with salt and pepper.

Put the steak on the grill and leave alone—let it cook for about 4 minutes (I like it more rare).

Flip and continue to cook until it's where you want it.

Remove from the grill and cover with foil—let it rest for 10 minutes.

Transfer to a plate and add a couple tablespoons of the blue cheese crumbles and a good drizzle of olive oil—this is where you want a really good olive oil.

And speaking of "on sale," ask the meat and seafood people at your store what's coming up to be on sale, because they usually know and will tell you. So instead of buying a lesser cut today, you might wait 'til tomorrow and buy a great piece of meat for less. This also applies to other stores too. See a pair of shoes you want? Ask about a sale . . . you never know what's on the horizon. And my last piece of advice (before my editor, Justin, kicks my ass for being way too off-topic) is that if you bought something today at regular price, and notice it went on sale a day or two or three later, go to the store with your receipt and ask for the difference to be refunded to you. Simply making the point that a clerk should have told you of an upcoming sale is usually enough to get the bucks back. Okay, back to the real topic at hand.

Adding something to a steak often takes it to a whole new level. And much like the blue cheese crumbles on the filet does it for me, other things are also fabulous additions. Need some ideas? Here you go:

Béarnaise Sauce—Think Hollandaise, but without the lemon and with a bunch of herbs added. But unlike Hollandaise that is meant for fish and vegetables, Béarnaise is really meant for meat. Make your life easy and buy a "just add water & butter" package of it.

Crab—A steak with lump crabmeat on top is very good. A steak with crabmeat and then Béarnaise sauce is absolutely insane. You must…

Onion Rings—Don't dis the lowly ring. A little stack of these with a small drizzle of BBQ sauce is crazy good.

Pepper—I don't mean in the usual "Kosher salt & pepper" way. I mean lightly oil a steak, season with salt. And then "grind an assload of fresh pepper onto a plate and press both sides of the steak into it before cooking" way.

Sautéed Mushrooms—Oh yes, a big whack of beautifully softened mushrooms on top is killer. Check the recipes on page 120.

Steak Butters—See page 48.

Simple Grilled Asparagus—Drizzle with olive oil and throw them on the grill for about 7 minutes.

Roasted Chilies—Throw some Anaheim chilies on the grill about 15 minutes before your steaks go on. Blacken on all sides, then put them in a bowl and cover with cling wrap. Let them sit maybe 10 minutes, peel off the skins, slice open, discard the seeds and membrane and chop roughly and add to the top of your steak.

Grilled Onions—Lightly oiled, seasoned and cooked on the grill, or sautéed in a pan. Either way, they add a ton of great flavor to a steak.

Any kind of salsa—A nice touch.

Steak Pizzaiola—This is essentially a steak with a zesty tomato sauce. So your favorite tomato sauce, could be warmed and added to the top of the steak.

chili rubbed tri-tip MAKES ONE 2- TO 3-POUND TRI-TIP

This is super simple and super good. A tri-tip is full of flavor and I love it. And because it's thick, remember for sure to take it out of the fridge about 30 minutes before grilling.

- 3 **tablespoons chili powder**
- 1 **tablespoon ground cumin**
- 1 **tablespoon dried oregano**
- 1 **tablespoon garlic powder**
- 1 **tablespoon kosher salt**
  Olive oil
- 1 **2- to 3-pound tri-trip, trimmed of most of the fat**

Preheat the grill to high.

Combine the chili powder, cumin, oregano, garlic powder and salt.

Drizzle the beef with olive oil, then sprinkle with spice mix and rub in well all over.

Place on the grill and cook until the desired doneness—for medium-rare, approximately 10 minutes a side.

Remove from the grill, cover with foil and let rest for about 15 minutes before slicing.

porterhouse with herb-garlic butter

MAKES 2

A porterhouse is a steak with a split personality—it's essentially 2 steaks in one. One side of a T-bone (see BTW) is a filet, and the other side is a New York—nice, huh? Almost the best of both worlds.

We're going to make this one using the Herb Garlic Butter, but of course you could use any herb butter that appeals to you. I figured if I didn't write out a recipe using one of the butters, you might not try them. So now you have to.

2   **porterhouse steaks**
    Olive oil
    Kosher salt and freshly ground black pepper
    Herb-Garlic Butter (page 49)

Remove the steaks from the fridge about 30 minutes before grilling.

Preheat the grill to high.

Lightly brush with oil and season with salt and pepper.

Grill on both sides until done to your liking, remove from the grill, and add a couple ⅛-inch slices of the butter. Cover and let sit for 10 minutes before eating.

Enjoy.

A porterhouse is 2 steaks on either side of a T-bone, which is not to be confused with a T-bone steak. The terms are often used interchangeably, and they are close, but not exact. Both have a New York on one side and tenderloin on the other, but the T-bone has much less tenderloin. So if you go to buy them in a store and they are priced the same, you'll get more of the tenderloin for your money with the porterhouse than the T-bone. Got it?

the granddaddy of the steak world—a whole tenderloin of beef

When you buy a filet mignon at the store or order one in a restaurant, it was once part of a whole tenderloin. Think essentially a piece of meat about the size of your arm— from your elbow to your fingertips. And not only is it easier to cook one big steak than a bunch of smaller ones, it's generally cheaper too. But depending on where you buy, it can take a bit of cleaning up—meaning it may come with fat on it. But once you master this, it may be hard to go back to individual steaks.

our favorite company thing SERVES 10 TO 15

- 1 whole filet of beef, 4 to 5 pounds (see BTW)
- 6 cloves garlic, minced
- 2 tablespoons chopped fresh rosemary
- 2 teaspoons each kosher salt and freshly ground black pepper
- ⅓ cup olive oil

  Horseradish Cream (page 37), for serving

Remove the filet from the fridge about 45 minutes before cooking.

Preheat the grill to high.

Clean and trim the filet, removing the silverskin (see BBTW) and excess fat.

Combine the garlic, rosemary, salt, pepper, and olive oil in a small bowl; mix well. Rub the oil/garlic mixture all over the tenderloin.

Grill the filet on all sides until it's cooked to your liking (medium rare is perfect, so look for your thermometer to read 130°F; it's a big piece of meat and will definitely continue cooking for a bit after you take it off the grill).

Let it sit, covered, for 15 to 20 minutes before serving.

Serve with Horseradish Cream.

On the previous page, I referred to a whole tenderloin as looking like your arm, from the elbow to the fingers, and it does. But this means one end is much thicker than the other, and your goal is to keep things generally the same thickness when you cook them. So using the arm analogy, if you stretch out your arm with fingers fully extended then fold your fingers back into your palm, you'll see that you have created a much more even thing to cook (the filet, not your arm). You can do this 2 ways with the filet:

1. You can cut off the thin end and grill it separately (which I often do during the cooking of the whole tenderloin as a present to myself and whoever else is out there with me).
2. Tie the thin end back with string like you folded your fingers back.

If you don't or can't buy the filet cleaned, you'll need to trim it of the unnecessary fat, especially the silverskin which is a thin layer of silver-looking stuff. Simply put your knife under one end of the silverskin, horizontal to the filet, and slide along. It will take a bit of effort the first few times you do this, but you'll get it eventually, and it is truly worth it.

a crazy-good asian ribeye

I'm a guy who likes his ribeye (see BTW) plain—just kosher salt and pep-per, but I made this for friends once and they loved it, so here you go. And it goes without saying that this will work with any kind of steak, I just happened to have made it with a ribeye.

- **4 boneless ribeye steaks**
- **1 cup soy sauce**
- **½ cup honey**
- **¼ cup minced fresh garlic**
- **¼ cup minced fresh ginger**
- **3 tablespoons dry mustard**
- **3 tablespoons five-spice powder**

Remove the steaks from the fridge and put in a casserole dish.

Mix together the soy sauce, honey, garlic, ginger, mustard, and five-spice powder. Spread on the steaks to coat well and let sit about 30 minutes.

Preheat the grill to high.

Remove the steaks from the marinade and grill until done to your liking—remove from the grill and let rest for 10 minutes.

Slice the steaks, and how about serving them with the Wasabi Mashed Potatoes on page 112?

AKA a "Del-monico" or "Spencer" steak, a ribeye has extra marbling, which means it also has extra fat, which means it also has extra flavor. And of course the extra fat means my wife Kelly will extra hate it.

sweet & spicy flank SERVES 4

A good flank steak is one of my favorite things. Just remember you have a day of marinating ahead of you before you can eat it . . .

- 8 ounces orange juice
- 3 ounces canned chipotle peppers in adobo sauce
- ½ cup brown sugar
- 1 bunch green onions, white and light green parts only
- 1 small bunch cilantro, top leaves only
- 1 flank steak, about 2 pounds

Put the orange juice, chipotle peppers with sauce, brown sugar, green onions, and cilantro in a food processor or blender and whirl until smooth.

Add the mixture and the flank steak to a zipper-top plastic bag, seal, and marinate in the refrigerator overnight.

Remove the bag from the fridge 30 to 45 minutes before grilling. Preheat the grill on high.

Remove the steak from the marinade and grill for about 5 minutes on each side for medium rare.

Slice into thin strips across the grain to serve.

Since you'll be standing at the grill, cooking two flanks will take no more time than cooking one, right? So I suggest you make two—and then use the extra for any of the things in the "What to Do with Leftover Steak" section on page 147.

carne asada SERVES 4

One of the best things you can do with a flank. I suggest cooking two of them so you'll have some leftover for tacos, breakfast burritos or the Carne Asada Fries on page 67.

- ⅓ cup olive oil
- ½ cup chopped cilantro
- 4 large cloves of garlic, minced
- 2 teaspoons ground cumin
  Grated zest and juice of 1 lime
  Kosher salt and freshly ground black pepper
- 1 2-pound flank steak

Combine the olive oil, cilantro, garlic, cumin, lime zest and juice, salt and pepper—mix well.

Put the flank and marinade into a large zipper-top plastic bag and let sit in fridge for 1 to 4 hours.

Remove flank from fridge about 30 minutes before cooking.

Preheat the grill to high.

Take the flank out of the marinade and cook for about 5 minutes per side for medium-rare.

Remove from the grill, cover with foil, and let sit about for 15 minutes Slice across the grain to serve.

big-ass shrimp & steak with chimichurri SERVES 4

Chimichurri is a garlic-parsley marinade that originated in Argentina—and it rules. Make sure you reserve some of the sauce (don't use it all for marinating) for dipping or drizzling.

CHIMICHURRI SAUCE

- 1 cup olive oil
- ⅓ cup red wine vinegar
- ¼ cup fresh oregano leaves
- 1 bunch flat-leaf parsley, top leaves only
- 6 cloves garlic
  Juice of 1 lemon
  freshly ground black pepper and ½ teaspoon each kosher salt

STEAK

- 4 8- to 10-ounce steaks
- 16 really big shrimp, shelled and deveined with the tail left on (U10s would be great)

Add the olive oil, vinegar, oregano, parsley, garlic, lemon juice, salt, and pepper to a blender or food processor and blend until smooth.

Place the steaks and shrimp in a shallow dish and cover with chimichurri sauce, reserving some sauce separately for serving.

Place in the refrigerator to marinate for 30 to 60 minutes.

Remove the dish from the fridge 30 minutes before grilling. Preheat the grill on high.

Take the steaks from the marinade and grill until done, about 5 minutes a side, remove, and cover with foil.

Add the shrimp to the grill, basting with some of the extra marinade.

Grill until beautifully done, which will be maybe 3-ish minutes a side and remove.

Slice the steak into thin slices and serve with the shrimp and the reserved extra chimichurri sauce for dipping.

garlic mustard steak SERVES 4

Just a great, big flavor event.

½ cup spicy brown mustard
8 cloves garlic, minced
2 tablespoons Worcestershire sauce
1 teaspoon dried thyme
4 New York steaks, or whatever steaks you like
    Kosher salt and freshly ground black pepper

Mix together the mustard, garlic, Worcestershire, and thyme—reserve a little for brushing the cooked steaks.

Season the steaks with salt and pepper, then brush both sides of the steak with the mustard mixture. Save some for serving. Allow to sit about 30 minutes.

Preheat the grill to high.

Grill the steaks until they are the desired doneness, about 5 minutes per side for medium rare.

When you remove the steaks from the grill, brush with the mustard mixture you reserved and then serve.

korean short ribs—kalbi SERVES 4

This is in the category of "don't cook the same stuff all the time." Make 'em once, and they'll be on your party lineup.

- 1½ cups soy sauce
- ½ cup sugar
- 6 large cloves garlic, minced fine
- 8 green onions, chopped small
- 1 tablespoon sesame oil
- 1 tablespoon freshly ground black pepper
- 5 pounds Korean short ribs (see BTW)

Combine the soy, sugar, garlic, green onions, sesame oil, and pepper in a bowl and mix well.

Add the mixture with the ribs to a big zipper-top plastic bag and mix to combine. Marinate for a couple hours or up to 1 day in the refrigerator.

Remove the meat from the refrigerator 30 minutes before cooking. Preheat the grill to medium-high heat.

Remove the meat from the marinade and grill for 2 to 3 minutes on each side.

Because these are quite thin, I like to serve them right away.

Korean short ribs can be purchase from an Asian market, but your meat guy can also prepare them for you. Instead of beef ribs being cut individually, imagine them being cut into ½-inch thick slices across the bones—so in each one you see a cross section of three bones. Get it?

what to do with lefover steak

You've prepped, you grilled, you've eaten, and now you have leftovers. What to do, what to do—what a great problem to have, right? The solutions are limitless, but here are a few favorites . . .

The concept of leftover steak applies just as nicely to leftover "anything." And considering cooking two things is almost as easy as one, you should think about throwing an extra whatever on the grill the next time you're out there. The next day, **you'll be very happy you did.**

amazing leftover steak tacos MAKES 8 TACOS

This requires not much more than the following, and since I don't know what you've got left, I'll merely suggest the necessary items—you can do this.

- 1 tablespoon olive oil
- 1 pound leftover steak, thinly sliced
- 1 teaspoon chili powder
- 8 corn tortillas
- ⅓ cup sour cream
- Something crunchy for contrast—cabbage, shredded carrots, thinly sliced red peppers
- Hot sauce

Get the olive oil pretty hot in a nonstick pan and toss in the leftover steak and chili powder. The key is not to overcook the steak, just get it all sizzling and glistening.

Warm the tortillas.

Add some sour cream to a tortilla, top with the crunchy stuff, then add the steak and a little hot sauce.

Booya.

steak salad with goat cheese & crispy tortillas SERVES 2

¼ cup olive oil
¼ cup finely chopped fresh cilantro
    Juice from 1 lime
2 teaspoons white wine vinegar
    Kosher salt and freshly ground black pepper to taste
2 flour tortillas, cut into thin matchsticks
8 ounces mixed greens
    About a pound of leftover steak, sliced thin
1 cup goat cheese

Combine the oil, cilantro, lime juice, vinegar, and salt and pepper—mix well and set aside.

Put tortilla pieces in a nonstick pan over medium heat, and cook until beginning to brown and getting crispy.

Put the greens in a bowl and add just enough dressing to lightly coat.

Plate the greens and top with the sliced steak. Crumble the goat cheese over the top and add the tortilla matchsticks. Serve.

night grilling

You come home after a day of hard work or hard play and are dying to grill up those thick steaks you bought yesterday. You take the steaks out of the fridge (because I've taught you not to cook them cold) . . . put on some good music, change into your relaxing clothes, open a bottle of wine, and since you have a little time, you sit down to share the highlights of your day with your significant other. Life is good.

But when you finally realize it's time to grill, you also realize it's gotten dark outside. **Damn—night grilling . . . again.**

Well, if you have lights on your grill, then you're still in business. But if like most of the grilling world . . . you don't, then what? Then you have some choices.

❄ Choice #1 Don't grill at all. Make your apologies and retreat to the oven or pan. But are you really doing justice to those amazingly thick dry-aged filets? I think not.

❄ Choice #2 Grill in the dark. And before you completely dismiss this as just a whacked idea, I've done it, you've probably done it, and a lot of people have done it. Of course you never intend to. It just happens and then you're @#$%.

❄ Choice #3 Get some light—any light. Even though you may have outside lights, they somehow never seem to be good enough or in the right spot. So keep a flashlight with fresh batteries always at the ready. Or, in a real emergency, the light of a cell phone will do. Hey, it's not ideal, but coming back inside with half-cooked whatever is not ideal either.

But there are 2 real fixes:

❄ Plan better. I know for me that's not usually possible. I am what I am, and pre-planning is not really part of my makeup—and that's why I have a "flashlight" app on my phone.

❄ Get a grill light. It's a simple little battery-operated contraption that clips onto the side of your grill and lights up your grill world. Now you're talking. I mean, now I'm talking.

> **Food cooked outside just tastes different than food cooked inside. Not necessarily better—just different. Okay, sometimes better. In fact, sometimes a lot better.**

There's just some-thing wonderful about standing over the grill, tongs in hand, watching what the flames can do to the food."

not beef.

juicy.

great

name, huh? I love a chapter title that leaves nothing to the imagination. For me, "not beef" says it all, and this chapter has it all—pork, chicken, lamb— all my faves. So don't just sit there—bust into it and make something.

pork "jerked" tacos MAKES 8 TACOS

"Jerk" seasoning, traditionally used in Jamaican cooking, can be a combination of anywhere up ten spices. Allspice is often used—I don't keep allspice. Cloves are often used—I don't keep cloves either, and it goes on. So being the simple fellow I like to be, I find it easier to just buy jerk seasoning already mixed from the market. All the flavor with none of the hassle of keeping a bunch of things you probably won't use for anything else.

- 2 **tablespoons jerk seasoning**
- 1 **tablespoon olive oil**
- 1 **pork loin filet, about 1½ pounds**
- 8 **corn tortillas, warmed**
  Grilled Pineapple Salsa (page 118), for serving

Combine the jerk seasoning and oil. Mix well. Rub the mixture all over the pork and let it sit for 30 minutes.

Preheat the grill to medium-high.

Put on the pork and cook until done, approx 140 to 145°F or about 12 to 15 minutes, turning every couple minutes.

Remove the pork from the grill, cover with foil, and allow to rest for about 10 minutes.

Slice thin and serve on the corn tortillas with the pineapple salsa.

I like to make an extra one or two of these to use in the Grilled Cuban (page 105).

horseradish pork tenderloin SERVES 6

You'll dig this—I like its crispy, burnt edges. Oops, you can't see it yet, can you? Guess you'll just have to take my word for it then . . .

 1 cup orange marmalade
1½ tablespoons soy sauce
1½ tablespoons Dijon mustard
1½ tablespoons prepared horseradish
 2 1-pound pork tenderloins
    Kosher salt and freshly ground black pepper

Preheat the grill to high.

Combine the marmalade, soy sauce, mustard, and horseradish and mix well. Set aside some of the sauce for drizzling on the pork at the end and use the rest for basting.

Season the pork with salt and pepper.

Grill the pork, turning to brown it well on all sides, then turn the heat to medium. Begin basting the pork once the heat is turned down—too soon and the sweet sauce will burn.

Continue cooking and basting until the pork is the way you like it—which for me is just a tiny bit pink in the center, about 140 to 145°F, or approximately 10 to 12 minutes.

Remove from the grill and allow the pork to rest for a few minutes.

Slice the pork. Warm the reserved marmalade and drizzle over the sliced pork; serve.

five-spice grilled chicken SERVES 6

Five-spice adds an insane amount of flavor for just one simple ingredient. And when it's combined with soy, brown sugar, and the lowly chicken thigh, something magical happens. What, too dramatic?

⅓ cup brown sugar
½ tablespoon five-spice seasoning
1 cup low-sodium soy sauce
3 pounds boneless, skinless chicken thighs, trimmed of extra fat
1 bunch green onions, diced very fine

Combine the brown sugar and five-spice in a bowl, then stir in the soy and mix really well.

Add the chicken and mix really, really well so it is all well covered.

Cover and marinate for at least a half hour, or up to overnight in the refrigerator.

If the chicken was refrigerated, remove it from the fridge 30 minutes before you plan to cook. Preheat the grill to high.

Cook the chicken on the grill until done but not too long or it will dry out, 5 to 6 minutes a side.

Remove the chicken from the grill, top with the green onion confetti, and enjoy.

chili-rubbed chicken with grilled avocados SERVES 4

Our friends Greg and Ginger are avocado farmers. Actually it's just Greg who's the farmer (Ginger is an attorney), but if I don't mention her she'll be pissed and sue me or something. Anyway, I shot a show at their really, really beautiful property and made this—and we all loved it. And I'll admit that grilled avocados sound kinda creepy, but they're actually really good.

⅓ cup chili powder
⅓ cup brown sugar
    Olive oil
8   boneless chicken thighs, roughly 2 pounds
    Kosher salt
2   avocados, pit removed, flesh scooped out and quartered
    Freshly ground black pepper

Combine the chili powder, brown sugar, and enough olive oil to make a thick paste.

Preheat the grill to medium.

Season the chicken with salt, then brush the chili paste on both sides. Put the chicken on the grill and start cooking.

When you flip the chicken after about 8 to 10 minutes, drizzle the avocado quarters with oil, season with salt and pepper, and put on the grill.

Cook the chicken on the second side until done. Turn the avocados carefully so they get color on all sides. Remove everything from the grill.

Serve the avocados alongside the chicken with an extra drizzle of olive oil.

Simple salted and grilled avocados make a great addition to almost anything you cook outside.

mustard, honey, & curry chicken thing

SERVES 4

Once again, another not-so-great name—but a so-great recipe. The day
we shot it for the show, it was essentially inhaled by the crew (Michelle
and Shannon) after. They ate like truckers.

½ **cup Dijon mustard**

⅓ **cup honey**

½ **cup chopped cilantro**

3 **tablespoons curry powder**

2 **pounds boneless chicken thighs**

2 **tablespoons olive oil**

Kosher salt & freshly ground black pepper to taste

Preheat the grill to medium.

Combine the mustard, honey, cilantro and curry powder—mix well and set
aside, reserving some of it for drizzling before serving.

Drizzle the chicken lightly with oil, then season with salt & pepper.

Grill the chicken for 5 to 7 minutes per side and begin basting with the mustard sauce on the cooked side once you flip it over.

Continue painting on the mix, on both sides until done.

Serve with an extra little drizzle of the sauce.

grilled lamb kebobs MAKES 6

Grilled ground lamb with a totally simple, but fantastic mint yogurt sauce—so, so good.

1 cup plain yogurt, Greek-style if possible (it's thicker and more bitchin')
3 tablespoons chopped fresh mint
  Grated zest of 1 lime
1 pound ground lamb
  Kosher salt and freshly ground black pepper
½ teaspoon ground cumin
6 wooden skewers, soaked in water about 30 minutes
  Olive oil
1 large tomato, diced
½ red onion, diced
6 pitas

Combine the yogurt, mint, and lime zest and set aside.

Preheat the grill to medium-high.

Season the ground lamb with salt and pepper, then mix in the cumin. Mold the lamb into 6 hot dog–shaped tubes around the top half of each skewer.

Brush the meat lightly with oil, add to the grill, and cook, turning often, until cooked through, about 10 minutes total.

As the lamb cooks, combine the tomatoes and onion and set aside.

When the lamb is done, remove from the grill and put the pitas on the grill to warm. Remove the pitas from the grill, spread some yogurt sauce on each pita, then add a lamb kebob and some of the tomato-onion mixture.

honey soy lamb chop MAKES ONE FULL RACK

The honey makes this marinade into a kind of glaze once it's grilled. The day we shot the pictures of this, Steve (the photographer) went home and had to make it for his own dinner that night—he thought it was that good. I like to cook the rack whole and then cut it into double chops.

- ½ **cup soy sauce**
- ½ **cup honey**
- 2 **cloves garlic, crushed**
- ½ **teaspoon cayenne pepper**
- 1 **Frenched rack of lamb (see BTW), rinsed and patted dry**
- 2 **tablespoons finely chopped fresh cilantro**

Mix together the soy, honey, garlic, and cayenne in a dish or zipper-top plastic bag.

Add the lamb and let marinate up to an hour. But, if you only have 10 minutes—cool, or if you have more time . . . that's better.

Preheat the grill to medium-high.

Remove the lamb from the marinade and add to the grill. Because it's on the rack still, you kind of end up with 3 sides—don't forget about the bottom. Cook for about 5 minutes on each side, until medium rare. Remove and let rest for 10 minutes, then cut into 2's.

Garnish with the chopped cilantro and serve.

A frenched rack of lamb just means that the fat and stuff between and around the protruding rib bones has been removed. It looks nicer and makes for a prettier presentation.

You can also wrap the exposed ribs with foil to prevent them browning on the grill and gettng a little ugly.

lamb with rosemary oil SERVES 4

I'm not exactly sure what the opposite of "to marinate" is, but this could be it. What I mean is that rather than put this lamb in a marinade to add flavor before it's cooked, you put it in the mixture after it's cooked. And because the meat is warm and still cooking a bit, it just pulls in all the flavors and makes for an amazing treat.

2   racks of lamb, cleaned (frenched) and cut in half (4 ribs each)
1   tablespoon olive oil
    Kosher salt and freshly ground black pepper
¾   cup olive oil
3   tablespoons finely chopped fresh rosemary
3   tablespoons finely chopped fresh basil
3   tablespoons finely minced garlic
1   tablespoon grated lemon zest

Preheat the grill to medium-high.

Lightly drizzle the lamb with the tablespoon of oil, and season well with salt and pepper.

Put the lamb on the grill and cook until done the way you like (and my fingers are crossed you're going with medium rare—about 12 to 15 minutes in total—and not well done)—lamb is amazing a little pink.

Combine ¾ cup of oil, the rosemary, basil, garlic, and lemon zest—mix well.

Take the lamb off the grill, stir the oil again, then immediately spoon some on both sides of the racks and serve right away.

sticky sweet ribs SERVES 4

So many people have written me about how much they love these ribs, that even though they were in my first book, *Just a Bunch of Recipes*, they definitely needed to be in this one. Just make them and you'll know why.

1½ cups plain barbecue sauce
¼ cup pancake syrup
¼ cup brown sugar
2 racks pork back ribs, about 4 pounds
¼ cup white vinegar

Mix the sauce, syrup, and brown sugar together and set aside.

Preheat the oven to 400°F.

Place the rib racks on a baking sheet or in a casserole dish large enough to hold them. Pour the vinegar onto the baking sheet or in the casserole dish and cover tightly with aluminum foil.

Bake for 75 minutes, or until very tender. Remove from the oven, carefully lift off the foil, and pour out the liquid—be very careful of the steam.

The ribs are now fully cooked and just need to be sauced and finished on the grill.

Preheat the grill to medium-high. Place the ribs on the grill, meat side down. Baste the back with the sauce.

Cook until they start to develop grill marks, about 5 minutes. Now turn over and baste the other side.

You could stop here after they grill a bit on this side, or you could baste them a bit more and then give them a couple more minutes, meat side down—that's what I do.

Give 'em one extra baste after they've been removed, and if not serving right away, one more just before you serve them.

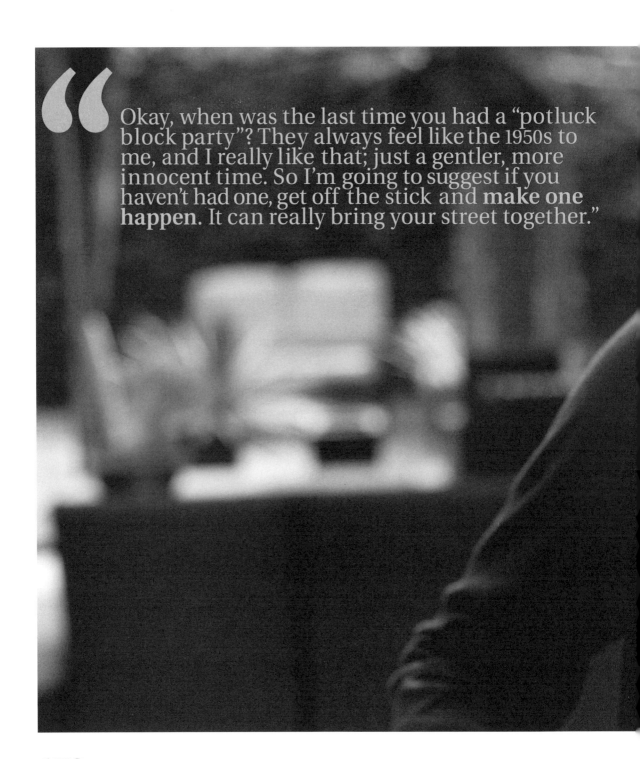

"Okay, when was the last time you had a "potluck block party"? They always feel like the 1950s to me, and I really like that; just a gentler, more innocent time. So I'm going to suggest if you haven't had one, get off the stick and **make one happen**. It can really bring your street together."

chinese bbq ribs SERVES 4

When it comes to ribs, people usually go old school. And by that, I mean traditional BBQ-saucy, chewin' on some straw, hangin' out in the barn with the farmer's daughter kinda ribs. Ya know? Well these are not like that. These are a little different, and I think you'll love 'em. If you're a beer person (and who isn't with ribs?), pick up a Chinese beer to go along with these.

2 racks pork back ribs, about 4 pounds
¼ cup white vinegar
½ cup soy sauce
⅓ cup honey
⅓ cup hoisin sauce
2 large cloves garlic, minced
2 teaspoons five-spice powder

Preheat the oven to 400°F.

Place the ribs and vinegar in a large baking or casserole dish. Cover tightly with aluminum foil and bake for 75 minutes, or until very tender.

Mix together the soy, honey, hoisin, garlic, and five-spice powder—set aside.

Remove the ribs from the oven and carefully lift off the foil—watch out for steam.

Preheat the grill to medium-high. Place the ribs, meat side down, on the grill. Baste the back with the sauce.

Cook until they start to develop grill marks and turn over—now baste the top. Baste a bit more while they finish and then one extra basting after they've been removed and just before you serve them.

seafood.

juicy.

might be my favorite chapter, simply because we eat a lot of seafood.

chinese grilled shrimp MAKES 10

That's kind of a lousy name for this recipe. What I mean are shrimp that are grilled and have an Asian flavor. Not shrimp that are grilled by—someone who's Asian . . . oh well.

- 10 wooden skewers
- 1 cup Asian salad dressing—something with sesame, ginger, etc. would be ideal
- 1 teaspoon red pepper flakes
- 1 pound impressively large shrimp (under 10s would be great), shell on and deveined

Put the skewers in a casserole dish and cover with water—let soak for about 30 minutes.

Put the dressing and pepper flakes in a bowl and mix well. Add the shrimp, stir to coat well, and let sit for about 20 minutes.

Preheat the grill.

Skewer the shrimp up through the tails so they stay straight.

Grill for 2 to 3 minutes per side, until done, then serve—still on their sticks

You could make this with pretty much any salad dressing—Greek, Italian, Canadian (whatever that would be)!

HOW TO GRILL FISH

Without standing there showing you what to do, I will share the tips I always share for this much discussed topic:

Don't let the fish psych you out—You're the one who's in charge. If you believe you can grill a piece of fish, you're halfway there.

Don't marinate fish too long or it'll get mushy—You can always baste during or add sauce after, but more than about 15 minutes is unnecessary.

Fish cooks quickly outside—Use medium-high heat and just go for it.

If it starts to stick, you're screwed—So make sure either the fish or the grill is well oiled—or both. Use an olive-oiled rag or a spray—they both work well. You could also use a fish basket—that would for sure prevent it from sticking, but it feels like cheating to me. I like the uncertainty and suspense of knowing I might screw up dinner.

You're looking for the fish to go opaque—If it's still translucent, it's likely not quite done. It'll get flaky when it's done—but you don't want too flaky or it'll be dry.

grilled catfish sandwich MAKES 2 SANDWICHES

Pickled mayonnaise and grilled catfish… it's like a bit of the South right where you are. Unless you're already there, then it's like… oh never mind.

- 2 8-ounce catfish fillets
- 2 tablespoons olive oil
- 2 tablespoons Old Bay Seasoning
- 2 ciabatta buns, long enough to hold the fillets
- 2 dill pickles
- ½ cup mayonnaise
- 1 tomato, sliced

Preheat the grill to medium-high.

Drizzle both sides of the catfish with olive oil and season with Old Bay.

Grill the catfish, 4 to 5 minutes a side.

While it cooks, dice the pickles and mix with the mayonnaise.

Slice the buns in half and grill until crispy and lightly golden brown.

Spread pickle-mayo on the toasted buns, then add tomato slices and then catfish. Add the top bun.

Eat.

snapper puttanesca SERVES 4

A staple in the camping world, cooking in foil is not just easy, but the steam cooks everything really well, keeps it moist, and helps add a ton of flavor. It's also fun to let people build their own.

    Aluminum foil
½ **cup olive oil**
1½ **pounds red snapper—in 4 small fillets**
    Kosher salt and freshly ground black pepper
4 **medium vine-ripened tomatoes, coarsely chopped**
½ **cup kalamata olives, pitted and coarsely chopped**
¼ **cup capers, optional—wait, make that not optional**
2 **cloves garlic, minced**
2 **teaspoons dried thyme**

Preheat the grill to medium.

Cut 4 sheets of foil about 20 inches long—fold each sheet in half. Drizzle a little oil on the center of each folded sheet, then add the fish. Season with salt and pepper.

Combine the tomatoes, olives, capers, garlic, and thyme in a small bowl.

Top each piece of fish with some of the tomato mixture. Drizzle with the remaining oil.

Fold the foil over the fish, closing up and pinching the edges to seal tightly.

Place the packets on the grill and cook for 15 to 20 minutes, or until the fish is opaque in the middle—which you won't see since they're sealed up, so you'll have to trust me on the time, and if it's wrong for your grill, adjust it next time.

Put them on plates and let your guests open the packets them-selves—just warn them of potential steam.

You can have these all prepped, sealed, and ready to grill, waiting in your fridge. Just remember to take them out about 30 minutes before you plan on grill-ing them. Okay?

grilled tuna salad SERVES 4

I love tuna because it's delicious, it's healthy, and it's often on sale. And in the middle of grill season, there's nothing better than a big-ass grilled-up tuna salad.

½ pound green beans, trimmed of ugly ends
4 6- to 8-ounce tuna steaks
½ cup soy- or ginger-based bottled salad dressing
8 cups mixed salad greens
½ cup chopped fresh cilantro
4 medium tomatoes, cut into wedges
1 English or Japanese cucumber, thinly sliced
Freshly ground black pepper

English and Japanese cucumbers do not have to be seeded or peeled. Cool, huh?

Preheat the grill to medium-high.

Put the green beans in a small bowl, add a tablespoon or two of water, and cover with plastic wrap. Microwave until they are cooked but still crisp tender, about 4 minutes. Remove and let cool.

Brush the tuna with some of the salad dressing. Grill the tuna for 2 to 3 minutes on each side until medium rare—you can watch as they cook and when they change color about one-fourth of the way up on the first side, flip. Do the same on side two, then remove and cut into ½-inch slices.

Mix together the salad greens, cilantro, cooled green beans, tomatoes, and cucumber in a large bowl and add dressing to your liking. Put on 4 plates.

Top the salad with sliced tuna, drizzle with a little more dressing, and add freshly ground black pepper.

scallop & shrimp ceviche SERVES 4 TO 6 AS AN APPETIZER

Not grilled or cooked in any traditional sense, but marinating in the lime juice changes the physical properties of the scallops and shrimp and turns them firm and opaque as if they had been cooked with heat—cool, huh? This is a great appetizer or starter to any meal being done outside.

½ pound sea scallops, diced small

½ pound raw shrimp, peeled and also diced small

1 cup lime juice (from 6 to 8 limes)

   Grated zest of 2 limes

½ cup chopped fresh cilantro

2 medium red chiles, diced small

½ cup cucumber, peeled, seeded, and diced small

2 avocados, diced small

   Something crunchy for serving—potato chips, tortilla chips, broken tostadas (see BTW)

In a bowl, combine the scallops, shrimp, lime juice and zest, cilantro, chiles and cucumber—mix well and make sure there's enough juice to cover. If not, add more.

Cover and refrigerate for anywhere from a couple hours to overnight.

Remove from the fridge, add diced avocado, and mix carefully so as not to mush the avocado. Serve with a slotted spoon so you don't get liquid, just the good junk.

This will sound weird, but my friend Maxine suggested I take a plain tostada, spread a thin layer of mayo on it, then put the ceviche on top of that and eat it. Totally odd sounding, but really, really good.

cedar plank salmon SERVES 6

Also from book one—I told myself any grill book I did, this would be in it. You can find the untreated cedar planks at your local lumberyard for very little money, or at a cookware store or supermarket for a lot more money—your choice.

1 cedar plank (dimensions are up to you, but about ¾ of an inch thick and big enough to fit the salmon with at least an inch of border, but not too big to fit on your grill)
1 whole salmon fillet
Olive oil
Kosher salt and freshly ground black pepper
2 to 3 cups brown sugar
Spray bottle of water, just in case

Soak the plank in water for at least 2 hours.

Preheat the grill to high for at least 15 minutes.

Place the salmon on the plank (skin side down if it has skin) and rub the top lightly with oil. Season well with salt and pepper. Cover the salmon with the brown sugar—and when I say "cover," I mean so you don't see any salmon . . . just brown sugar.

Place the board with the salmon on the heated grill and close the lid. For a fillet about an inch at its thickest and depending on how good your barbecue is, it will take maybe 12 to 15 minutes to cook. The plank sides may flare up during cooking (this is what the bottle of H_2O is for). This is no big deal as long as you keep the salmon about an inch away from the edges.

Carefully remove the plank from the grill and serve.

btw

This salmon . . . the next day . . . all mixed up with a little mayo and some chili sauce and diced green onions is maybe the best salmon salad you'll ever have. It's crazy good.

whole grilled trout MAKES 1 TROUT

There are some things in this world we all need to try at least once—and grilling a whole fish is one of them. Not only is this simple and delicious, but is so bitchin' looking when you put it in front of your guests—they'll be way excited. And for those of you too young to know, "bitchin'" means very good.

- 1 whole trout, cleaned (see BTW)
  Extra virgin olive oil
- 2 garlic cloves, minced
  Kosher salt and freshly ground black pepper
  Small handful fresh herbs—basil, thyme, Italian parsley,
   oregano—whatever
- 1 lemon, sliced into ¼-inch-thick rounds

Preheat the grill to medium-high.

With a knife, make 3 or 4 diagonal cuts down each skin side of the fish—about ¼ inch of the way in.

Drizzle the inside of the fish with olive oil, rub in the garlic, then season with salt and pepper.

Scatter the herbs inside of the fish, add the lemon slices, and close.

Lightly oil the skin on both sides of the fish.

Grill for 5 to 6 minutes on each side, carefully flipping halfway through.

Remove and serve immediately.

I'm not a big "catch a fish and clean it yourself" kinda guy, so I take the easy approach. And that simply means buying a whole, cleaned trout from a fish market or from the seafood counter.

"something" with olive tapenade SERVES 4

Since this is the fish section, you should have figured out that the "something" is going to be some kind of fish, right? The thing is, I don't really mind what kind of fish you use here, as long as it is a white fish. It could be snapper, halibut, sea bass, or even shark—it won't really matter. It's just that most white fish have a little less of their own flavor and are nicely flavored by other things.

Olive oil
4 6- to 8-ounce "something" fillets
Kosher salt and freshly ground black pepper
¾ cup Olive Tapenade (page 21)
fresh chopped Italian parsley

Preheat the grill to medium.

Lightly oil the "something," then season with salt and pepper.

Grill for about 5 minutes a side—remember, the goal is moist, not dried out.

Remove from the grill and plate, adding some of the tapenade beautifully on top (with a little falling off the side for effect) and a good drizzle of olive oil. Sprinkle with chopped parsley.

snapper tacos SERVES 4

I'm a Southern California guy and we pretty much make tacos out of anything—so sue me. Snapper is usually thin and cooks pretty fast—just have all your stuff ready to go.

2	ripe avocados, diced
½	red onion, diced
⅓	cup chopped fresh cilantro
⅓	cup sour cream
1	tablespoon chili powder
1	tablespoon fresh lime juice
1½	pounds red snapper fillets
	Olive oil
	Kosher salt and freshly ground black pepper
8	6-inch corn tortillas

Preheat the grill to medium-high.

Mix together the avocados, onion, and cilantro—set aside.

Mix together the sour cream, chili powder, and lime juice—also set aside.

Lightly drizzle the snapper with oil and season with salt and pepper. Grill the snapper until just cooked through, maybe 6 to 8 minutes total. Then remove from the grill, cut into a rough chop, cover with foil, and keep warm.

Put the tortillas on the grill and cook on both sides until just beginning to get crispy.

Spread the sour cream mix on each tortilla and top with some snapper and then some of the avocado stuff—eat.

scallops with mayo'd teriyaki SERVES 6

This may sound odd, but mayo and teriyaki make an amazingly great combo, seriously. And with just a few steps, even if you hate it (which you won't), it's not like you went through a ton of work, right?

Wooden skewers
½ cup mayonnaise
2 tablespoons teriyaki sauce, store bought (try to make it a thick one)
18 large sea scallops (about a pound), defrosted
Kosher salt and freshly ground black pepper
Roasted white sesame seeds, for garnish, about a tablespoon

Cover the skewers with water and soak 30 minutes.

Preheat the grill to medium-high.

Combine the mayo and teriyaki sauce—mix well.

Skewer 3 scallops with 2 skewers—I find the second skewer keeps them from spinning—repeat with the remaining scallops.

Season lightly with salt and pepper and brush with the sauce.

Grill 2 for 3 minutes a side, brushing with sauce as they cook.

Remove, sprinkle with some sesame seeds, and serve.

So my own rule is not to add a sweet sauce until the last minutes of grilling because it might burn. But since these only take a few minutes a side, you need to start early—plus a few slightly burned teriyaki scallop edges will be delicious.

pesto—seafood's best friend

There are a handful of recurring items in my cookbooks—bacon, blue cheese, shrimp, bacon, and pesto. Pesto is one of those already-work-done multi-ingredient things you can buy that in a flash will add so much flavor. For example:

pesto scallops MAKES 12 SCALLOPS

I spoke about using pesto with shrimp in my first book, and as good as it is, I think it might be even better with scallops.

½ **cup store-bought pesto**
12 **sea scallops**

Preheat the grill to medium-high.

Brush or spoon the pesto on top of the scallops.

Put the scallops on the grill, pesto side down, and let cook until golden-y brown and good grill marks appear.

Brush the pesto on top and flip the scallops. Grill just until cooked through—and remember, you can eat scallops raw, so please don't over-cook the crap out of them.

These would totally fly as an appetizer course, or with some meat like a surf & turf kinda deal.

spicy grilled fish with pesto SERVES 4

If I haven't already mentioned it, I want you to feel free to try different things when you cook. All you need to know here is to keep some pesto around. Then pretty much whatever fish you have will work with it.

½ cup store-bought pesto
1 teaspoon red pepper flakes
4 6-ounce fillets, you choose
 Extra virgin olive oil
 Freshly ground black pepper

Preheat the grill to medium-high.

Mix the pesto with the pepper flakes.

Brush or spoon the pesto on top of the fish.

Put the fillets on the grill, pesto side down, and grill for about 5 minutes.

Brush the pesto on top of the fillets and flip. Continue grilling until cooked through, 3 to 4 more minutes, and remove carefully.

Top with a little more pesto, a drizzle of olive oil, and some freshly ground black pepper. Serve.

Pesto freezes really well, but trying to ice-pick a couple tablespoons out of a tub is a pain. So if you have ice cube trays, you can always buy pesto, spoon it into the trays, freeze them, and then put the cubes in a zipper-top plastic bag in the freezer. Then it's as simple as grabbing one or two cubes when you need them. Oh, and you can buy (or make) different kinds of pesto, like basil, cilantro, sun-dried tomato . . . you get it.

sea bass with lemon & capers SERVES 4

A caper is the salted and pickled bud from a plant—specifically the Capparis spinosa plant—and yes, that will be on the test. Anyway, it's a genius little thing that adds a great boost of flavor when you chomp it. And by chomp, I mean "bite."

- 4 tablespoons (½ stick) butter
- 1 big clove garlic, minced
- 3 tablespoons capers, drained
  Juice of 1 lemon
- 1 teaspoon grated lemon zest (you know that's just the yellow part, right?)
- 2 tablespoons chopped fresh basil
- 4 sea bass fillets, 6 to 8 ounces each
  Kosher salt and freshly ground black pepper

In a small pot, melt the butter over low heat, then add the garlic, capers, lemon juice, and zest. Simmer for about a minute, stir in the basil, and remove from the heat.

Season the fish with salt and pepper and drizzle with a little of the lemon-caper butter. Allow to sit for about 5 minutes.

Preheat the grill to medium-high.

Grill the sea bass about 5 minutes on the first side, then flip carefully and cook for another 3 to 4 minutes, or until it's the way you like it.

Remove from the grill, plate, add more of the lemon caper sauce, and serve.

"Why **people are scared of seafood** on the grill is beyond me. It cooks quick, is quite hardy, and requires very little seasoning. Now frying an egg—that scares the hell outta me . . ."

your everyday really good clams & mussels SERVES 4

This is one of the easiest, cheapest, and funnest party kinda things you can do with a grill (see BTW).

Yes I know "funnest" isn't proper English. It just sounded goodest there.

2 ounces "ready bacon," diced
  Large foil roasting pan
½ cup (1 stick) butter
1 cup dry white wine or vermouth
3 tablespoon minced garlic
1 teaspoon crushed red pepper flakes
2 pounds mussels, cleaned

2 pounds small clams, cleaned (littleneck clams are great, but don't go crazy looking cuz almost any clam will do, except that horrifying-looking arm-sized "geoduck" thing)
⅓ cup chopped fresh parsley

Preheat the grill to medium-high.

Place the foil roasting pan on the grill. Add the bacon, and let cook for about 5 minutes. Add the butter, wine (or vermouth), garlic, and pepper flakes.

When the butter has melted, stir to mix everything and when it's bubbling, add the mussels and clams and let the sauce come to a simmer. Cover the top with foil and close the grill lid.

Once the shells have all opened, approximately 8 to 10 minutes, stir everything well to coat with the sauce, add the parsley, and serve right out of the pan with some good bread for dipping.

Clam and Mussel Tip: You want to make sure the clams and mussels are alive. The shells should be closed tight, so if they're not, give them a quick rap on a counter. If they close up, they're fine. If they don't, give 'em to someone you hate. (My attorney has advised me to let you know that I was just kidding about giving bad clams and mussels to someone you hate. That is not something I would ever condone—and you should not do that. Toilet paper the #$%& out of their house, but don't give them bad shellfish.) To clean, give the outside a quick scrub with a stiff brush under running water to remove any dirt and any of the hairy stuff.

lobster tails with ginger butter SERVES 4

At some point you should try your hand at lobster, not just because it's really good, but because, well, you should just try everything once. Know what I mean? See BBTW.

½ cup (1 stick) butter, softened
⅓ cup well-minced fresh ginger
¼ chopped fresh cilantro
2 teaspoons chopped garlic
1 teaspoon sesame oil
 Pinch kosher salt
4 lobster tails (see BTW)

Combine the butter, ginger, cilantro, garlic, sesame oil, and salt—mix well and set aside.

Place the lobster tails, shell side down, on a cutting board, tail away from you.

Cut the undershell straight up the middle toward the tail—good kitchen shears are perfect for this.

Taking a knife, cut down into the meat partially to butterfly it but don't cut all the way through.

Because the tails have a tendency to curl up, I like to take a skewer and push it through the meat until it pokes back out just before the tail.

Preheat the grill to medium-high and spread some of the butter mixture on the meat of each tail.

Put the tails on the meat grill, side down, and cook for 4 to 6 minutes. Turn them over, add more butter to the top, and cook for another 3 to 4 minutes, or until done.

We have a large store near us (it rhymes with "Ostco") that often has previously frozen, but really nice, lobster tail for sale at a great price. Don't be afraid—just buy some and give 'em a go.

I'm not telling you what to do, but I'm guessing there are other things in your life you have been "hesitant" to do, and I say you should do them.

Life is way too short, and no one wants to get to the end and be like, "Wait a sec—I've missed out on that all these years?"

curried clams & mussels SERVES 4

There something about curry that I love—and there's something about curry that clams and mussels love. This is a marriage made in clam and mussel heaven.

Large foil roasting pan
½ cup (1 stick) butter
½ cup dry white wine or vermouth
1 cup whipping cream
8 green onions, green and light green parts only, chopped into ½-inch pieces
3 tablespoons minced garlic
1 tablespoon curry powder
2 pounds each mussels and clams, cleaned
⅓ cup chopped fresh cilantro

Preheat the grill to medium-high.

Place the foil roasting pan on the grill. Add the butter, wine (or vermouth), cream, green onions, garlic, and curry powder.

When the butter has melted, stir to mix everything well and when all is bubbling, add the mussels and clams and let the sauce come to a simmer. Cover the top with foil and close the grill lid.

Once the shells have all opened, after 8 to 10 minutes, stir everything well to coat with the sauce, add the cilantro, and serve right out of the pan

dogs &
burgers.

fun.

is such a happy title for a chapter (Dogs & Burgers) that I wanted to put one of those little happy faces beside it. If you've ever needed inspiration to do your own thing with hot dogs and hamburgers, this chapter should do it. After all, how can anything you do with a dog or burger be bad?

bacon-wrapped dog MAKES 6 DOGS

Leaving a Lakers game in Los Angeles one night, we stopped at a tiny stand selling a version of these. Actually, calling it a stand is going too far. It was more of a modified supermarket shopping cart—and the dogs were crazy good.

- 1 onion, cut into thin slices
- 2 green bell peppers, thinly sliced
- 1 tablespoon olive oil
- Kosher salt and freshly ground black pepper
- 6 kosher dogs (see BTW)
- 6 slices bacon
- 6 hot dog buns (good ones)

TO SERVE

Mayo

Diced jalapeños

Mustard

Diced tomatoes

Preheat the grill to medium-high.

In a nonstick pan over medium heat, cook the onion and peppers in the oil, stirring, until softened, about 7 minutes. Season with salt and pepper.

Wrap each dog with a piece of bacon and secure with toothpicks. Grill until the bacon is done—about 8 minutes. When the bacon is done, so is the dog—remove from the grill.

Lightly toast the buns on the grill. To serve, put some mayo on a bun, add the bacon dog, then add the onions and peppers. Add mustard, jalapeños, and diced tomatoes and serve.

I realize suggesting a kosher dog with the bacon sounds contradictory. But this is not about religious practice; this is about what goes into a kosher dog—or actually what *doesn't* go into them. The hot dog–making world is often filled with "odds & ends." You don't want what goes into many hot dogs. And without going into a long, usually gross description, a kosher dog is the way to go—you'll just need to trust me on this.

fry dog MAKES 6

A basic dog with a twist. Fry, as in "fries," not "fried," but "fries dog" would be poor grammar so I didn't use it.

6 kosher dogs
½ cup American chili sauce
¼ cup mayo
2 cups French fries, cooked following the package directions and tossed in seasoning salt when done
6 good hot dog buns

Preheat the grill to medium-high.

Cook the dogs on the grill until beginning to blister and looking great—remove from the grill.

Combine chili sauce and mayo, set aside.

Lightly grill buns, add some sauce and a dog, and top with fries.

Eat.

peppered coleslaw dog MAKES 6

(Try to read this sounding like Scarlett O'Hara, from Gone With the Wind.*)*

In parts of the southern United States, you'll find the popular "slaw dog" that's topped with a sweet, finely chopped, mayo-based slaw. This isn't one of those.

- 2 **cups ready coleslaw mix with sauce**
- 2 **tablespoons freshly ground black pepper—the pepper makes it**
- 6 **brats, fully cooked**
  Spicy brown mustard
- 6 **brat buns**

Preheat the grill to medium-high.

Mix together the coleslaw and pepper and set aside.

Cook the brats on the grill until beginning to blister and looking great—remove from the grill.

Toast the buns on the grill, then add mustard, and a brat, and top with the slaw.

pastrami reuben dog

I love a Reuben, and I always make it with coleslaw instead of sauerkraut. So it just makes sense that if I was going to turn it into a dog, I'd do the same.

6	kosher dogs
12	slices deli pastrami
6	good hot dog buns—if you can find dark rye ones, I say go for it
6	tablespoons spicy brown mustard
	Thousand Island dressing
6	slices Swiss cheese
1½	cups coleslaw—the premade deli kind is perfect

Preheat the grill to medium-high.

Cook the dogs until they are beginning to blister and looking great, and remove from the grill.

Put the pastrami and buns on the grill and cook for about a minute each side, until beginning to brown.

Serve by putting some dressing on each toasted bun, then add the hot dog, the mustard, the pastrami, then the cheese, and finally the coleslaw.

one pot brats MAKES 10 BRATS

A brat is basically the bully of the hot dog world. Big, bold, and brash—there's no question when a brat is in the room. And I love mine messy and even split open from the final cooking on the grill. A brat with attitude . . . beautiful. The simplest way is to take them right out of the package and throw them on the grill. But starting them in an onion beer bath is the gentlemanly way to go.

Large foil roasting pan
2 tablespoons olive oil
2 large yellow onions, thinly sliced
2 12-ounce bottles dark beer
⅓ cup brown sugar
2 tablespoons Worcestershire sauce

10 brats
2 tablespoons butter
Freshly ground black pepper
10 buns that will hold a brat

Preheat the grill to medium-high.

Place the foil roasting pan on the grill. Add the oil and then the onions and cook, stirring, until tender, 5 to 10 minutes.

Add the beer, brown sugar, and Worcestershire sauce. Bring to a boil, then reduce the heat to a simmer and add the brats. Close the lid and cook for 15 to 20 minutes.

Remove the brats from the beer bath and place the brats directly on the grill to brown.

Now, I like to pour off most of the beer from the foil, add the butter, lots of freshly ground black pepper, and cook the onions a bit more to serve on the brats.

Brown the buns on the grill, then add a brat to each bun and top with some of the onion stuff.

burger from the east MAKES 4

Beefy, Asian-y, and crunchy from the slaw. There's no bad here.

1¼ pounds ground beef
 2 cloves garlic, minced
 2 teaspoons minced fresh ginger
 1 bunch green onions, white and light green parts only, chopped fine
   Kosher salt and freshly ground black pepper
 ¼ cup hoisin sauce
 2 teaspoons Asian chili sauce
 1 small bag broccoli slaw
 ¼ to ⅓ cup mayonnaise
 1 teaspoon sesame oil
 4 buns, and make them kinda interesting, okay?

Mix together the beef, garlic, ginger, green onions, and salt and pepper well. Shape into patties.

Preheat the grill to medium-high.

Combine the hoisin and chili sauces and set aside.

Mix together the broccoli slaw, mayo, and sesame oil—set aside.

Cook the burgers to the desired doneness—about 5 minutes a side for medium-rare—brushing each side with the sauce once that side has been cooked, and then again when you take them off.

Grill the buns until light brown. To serve, put some extra sauce on a bun, then the burger, and then top with the slaw.

herbed honey dijon burger MAKES 4

Honey and Dijon, not just on the burger, but in the burger and all mixed up with a ton of herbs. Fanfrickingtastic.

- ¼ cup honey
- ¼ cup Dijon mustard
- 1½ pounds ground beef
- ½ cup finely chopped fresh herbs—any combo of thyme, parsley, basil, cilantro, and the like
-     Kosher salt and freshly ground black pepper
- 4 good buns
- 1 big handful arugula, or something leafy and green
- 2 large tomatoes, sliced in ¼-inch slices

Combine the honey and Dijon, mix well, and set aside.

Mix the beef with about a third of the honey mixture, and all the herbs, and season with salt and pepper. Combine well and shape into 4 patties.

Preheat the grill, or a cast-iron pan well.

Cook the burgers on the grill (or the pan) for about 5 minutes a side for medium rare, remove, and keep warm.

Lightly grill the buns, then top with the leafy green stuff, tomato slices, burgers, and then extra sauce. Add the bun tops.

Enjoy.

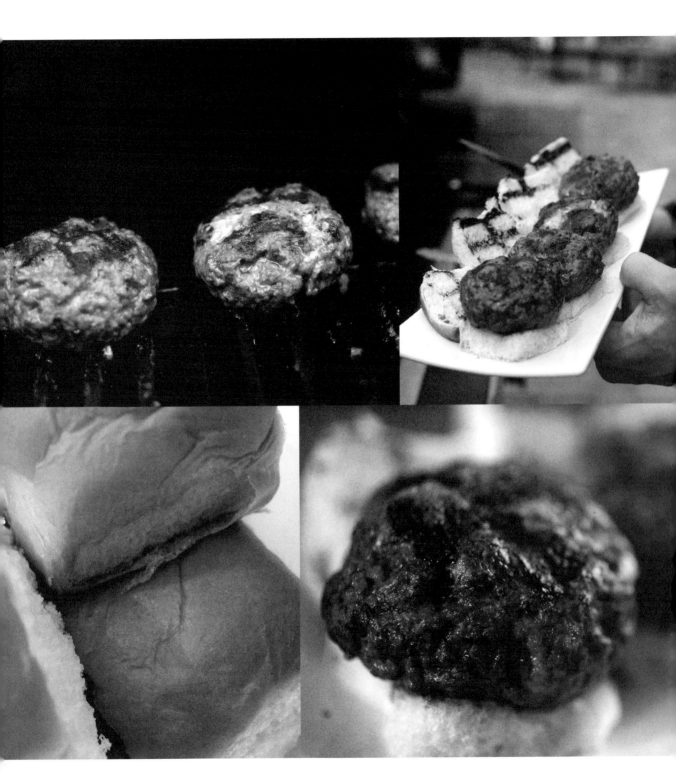

blue cheese stuffed sliders

Baby burgers . . . you can eat a ton of 'em cuz they're like having a snack.

1½ **pounds ground beef**
1 **to 2 teaspoons seasoning salt**
2 **ounces blue cheese crumbles**
2 **tablespoons butter, softened**
   Olive oil
   Freshly ground black pepper to taste
6 **small buns, like those little Hawaiian rolls**

Place the beef in a bowl, add the seasoning salt, and mix well. Split into 6 evenly sized burgers.

In a small bowl, combine the blue cheese, and butter and mix well. Make an indentation in the middle of each mini burger with your thumb and fill with some of the blue cheese mix. Fold the burger around the mix and seal well.

Lightly oil each patty and season with freshly ground black pepper. Preheat the grill to medium-high. Add the burgers and cook on each side for 3 to 4 minutes for medium-rare doneness. Remove from the grill.

Slice the buns open, grill until toasted, and make them into burgers—you know . . . bun, burger, bun—that sort of thing.

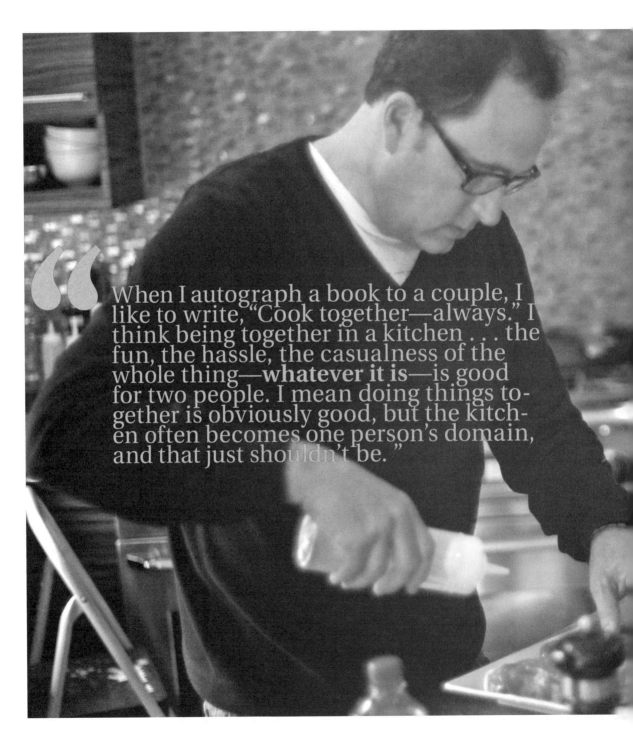

"When I autograph a book to a couple, I like to write, "Cook together—always." I think being together in a kitchen . . . the fun, the hassle, the casualness of the whole thing—**whatever it is**—is good for two people. I mean doing things together is obviously good, but the kitchen often becomes one person's domain, and that just shouldn't be."

veggie burger SERVES 4

I've always been amazed at what veggie burgers seemed to be made of—nuts, grains, beans, twigs, rocks, and sand that have been knocked out of the bottom of Birkenstock shoes (see BTW) . . . but where were the vegetables? Maybe somewhere, but in those preformed patties, it's really hard to tell. So mine are made of actual and totally legit vegetables—but don't end up being shaped into patties. Okay, call it creative license, but I'm sure you get that it doesn't have to be in a patty shape to be called a burger. I mean, hot dogs are not really in the shape of . . . oh, forget it.

- ⅓ cup store-bought pesto
- ⅓ cup softened goat cheese
- 2 large carrots, cut lengthwise into wide ¼-inch-thick strips
- 2 red bell peppers, sides cut off and core and seeds discarded
- 2 yellow peppers, sides cut off and core and seeds discarded
- 1 red onion, cut into ½-inch-thick rounds
- 1 large eggplant, cut into ½-inch-thick rounds
- Olive oil
- Kosher salt and freshly ground black pepper
- 4 sourdough buns (if you can find them, and if not, whatever works for you)

Preheat the grill to medium-high. Mix together the pesto and goat cheese—set aside.

Put the veggies on a platter or baking sheet, brush lightly with oil, and season with salt and pepper.

Transfer the veggies to the grill and cook on both sides until tender and a little charred all over—this will be 7 to 10 minutes total for the peppers and carrots and about 5 minutes total for the onion and eggplant.

Toast the buns lightly on the grill.

Spread the pesto mixture on the bottom of the buns and add the veggies and the top bun.

btw

Attention Vegan Activists: Please resist the urge to contact my publisher and rip on me for my "unfair" characterization of veggie burgers and for making fun of your shoe of choice. But really, have you guys tried some of the veggie burgers out there? I was actually being kind . . .

teriyaki mushroom-mushroom burger MAKES 4 BURGERS

I shot a show at the San Diego Zoo—wait, make that "the world-famous" San Diego Zoo. I felt like cooking with meat would have been in poor taste, and my sister-in-law Cheryl suggested I make something with portobello mushrooms, so I did . . . and I loved it.

1 pound sliced white button mushrooms
   Olive oil
⅓ cup teriyaki sauce, plus extra for serving
4 portobello mushrooms—the big guys, right?
8 slices Monterey Jack cheese
4 whole wheat buns
   Mayonnaise
2 ripe medium tomatoes, cut into 8 slices

Put the sliced mushrooms and about 1 tablespoon of the oil in a nonstick pan and cook, stirring occasionally over medium heat, until softened, about 5 minutes. Add the teriyaki sauce, mix, and turn off the heat.

Preheat the grill to medium-high.

Lightly drizzle the portobellos with oil, place on the grill, and cook for 3 to 4 minutes on each side until softened. Add 2 slices of cheese to each portobello and put the buns on the grill.

While the cheese melts and the buns toast, reheat the teriyaki mushrooms if necessary.

Once the bottom buns are toasted, add some mayo and a little teriyaki sauce and then tomato slices. Place the portobellos on top, then the sliced mushrooms and the top bun.

Eat.

the fried egg turkey burger MAKES 4 BURGERS

Turkey—good for you, right? Of course. But then turkey, dry as toast in a burger sometimes, is also right. So the addition of the fried egg and softened onions keep that from happening. It's delicious and you still feel good about yourself.

- 1 tablespoon olive oil
- 1 large red onion, the bigger the better, sliced thin
- 1½ pounds ground turkey
- 1 tablespoon steak seasoning
- ⅓ cup barbecue sauce
- 4 large eggs
- 1 tablespoon butter
- 4 English muffins, split

Heat a nonstick skillet to medium, add the olive oil and the onions—cook, stirring until nicely caramelized, about 10 minutes.

In a bowl, mix the turkey with the seasoning and 1 tablespoon of the barbecue sauce. Separate the turkey mixture into 4 equal portions and form into patties.

Preheat the grill to medium-high.

Grill the burgers until nicely charred on both sides and cooked through, 4 to 6 minutes a side.

In a nonstick pan over medium heat, cook the eggs in the butter—I like to go over-easy cuz there's just something about the yolk running down through the onions, burger, etc.

Meanwhile, grill the muffins until toasty. Top each bottom with a burger, onions, a fried egg, then the top of the bun.

If it isn't obvious, a fried egg can always be added to any burger (and should).

I realize turkey and steak seasoning may seem a bit . . . contradictory. But the turkey won't mind, and neither will you

pork loin burgers with curried slaw

MAKES 4

A burger doesn't have to be ground up. Pork loin chops work beautifully as a burger and go great with this curried slaw.

- 1 bag preshredded coleslaw (with the little pack of coleslaw dressing)
- 2 tablespoons curry powder
- 4 boneless pork loin chops
  Olive oil
  Kosher salt and freshly ground black pepper
- 4 crispy sandwich rolls
  Mayonnaise

Preheat the grill to high.

Combine the coleslaw, dressing mix, and curry powder—set aside.

Brush the chops lightly with oil and season well with salt and pepper.

Cook the chops on the grill until slightly charred and crispy on the outside but still moist inside, 4 to 6 minutes per side.

Grill the rolls. To each bun, add some mayo, the chops, and the slaw.

At this point I usually run around the house yelling loud enough for the neighbors to hear about how good these are. But my traditions don't have to be your traditions.

grilling inside.

easy.

I first sat down to write this book, I had every intention of including a chapter on indoor grilling. You know . . . what recipes you could do inside when you can't or don't want to cook outside. It was all so clear to me. But then a lot of things that make sense inside my head don't necessarily make sense on the outside.

And if my own issues weren't enough . . . I had an epiphany.

It wasn't the recipes that needed to be different—it was the equipment. Because the only thing you needed inside to get close to what you could do outside was a grill pan. You can cook a burger out, and you can cook a burger in. You can cook a steak out, and you can cook a steak in. But it's the grates of the grill that help give the distinctive flavor and look—and you can't get that in the oven or in a flat pan on the stove.

But with the raised searing ridges of the grill pan, you're golden. I made a steak tonight using one of my grill pans, and it was perfect. Not only does it work out nicely for the cooking part, but then I started thinking about the people who didn't have access to the outside. The tons of apartment dwellers living high above everyone all over the place. What do they do?

They can't possibly have room for a GrillMaster 8000 . . .

So they can do this: they can get a grill pan, and make everything in this book like the outside people do. Except they won't have to listen to the neighbors fighting, or be bothered by bugs, or run out of propane. The more I think about it, the better it sounds . . .
BTW, I love the name "The Outside People." I think it sounds like a Stephen King novel.

"

Get yourself a ridged grill pan and pull it out on a rainy winter day. Celebrate all your favorite summertime grilling items—only inside. Get a bucket of ice and fill it with some cold beers, put bathing suits on, apply suntan lotion (the smell of it will help with the illusion) . . .

And then invite a handful of close friends to celebrate with you. Don't let the weather tell you how to eat. You're the boss of you."

drinks &
desserts.

fun.

me admit that I didn't really know where to put some these recipes, so
I put them here. And the title Drinks and Desserts totally works, right?
Here's what it comes down to—I am sitting here right now, in a room in
my house, writing each and every word of this book. No ghost writer, no
assistants, no nothing. Just me in bad sweatpants, and flip-flops, unshav-
en with a sleeping dog beside me. So cut me some slack.

But as far as the desserts go, the grill is probably still warm as you're
finishing your dinner, so you might as well take advantage of its being
there and raring to go. BTW, I don't think I've ever written out the word
"raring" before. I should actually look it up to make sure it's spelled right,
hold on a second. I'm back and yes, it's correct:

> **raring (re(ə)ri ng)|**
> adjective |with infinitive| informal
> very enthusiastic and eager to do something: she was raring to get back to
> her work | the grill was raring to go.

So you've likely got a very enthusiastic and eager grill just sitting there.
Come on, let's do something with it . . . but we'll start with the drinks first.

pimm's cup MAKES 1

Pimm's is a gin-based alcohol created in London in 1840 by the owner of a London oyster bar. It can be mixed with 7up, lemonade, or in this case, ginger ale. It's super-refreshing for grilling season and easily one of my favorites.

Ice
2 parts Pimm's
2 parts ginger ale
1 slice or wedge orange
1 long cucumber spear

Fill a glass with ice and add Pimm's and ginger ale.

Squeeze and drop in the orange slice or wedge. Add the cucumber to stir, then leave it in, and drink.

The cucumber should not be viewed as merely a garnish. It's more than that and really adds to the overall fresh taste. Don't leave it out.

vodka cucumber mojito MAKES 1

Cucumber in almost any drink makes it "uber" refreshing. And this is no different.

1 ¾-inch piece of cucumber, peeled
1 teaspoon sugar
4 mint leaves (see BTW)
   Ice
2 ounces vodka
   Soda
   Lime wedge, for garnish

Drop the cucumber, sugar, and mint in a tall glass. Using the handle of a wooden spoon or a muddler, or the top of a bottle of wine, or your hammer handle, mash up everything.

Add the ice and vodka and top off with the soda.

Squeeze and drop in the lime wedge.

Feel free to add an extra sprig or two of mint as a charming garnish before serving. I choose not to because you take a sip and end up with a mouthful of leaves, but hey—it's up to you.

french on the rocks (FRANÇAIS SUR LES ROCHES)

FAIT UN (MAKES 1)

One of Kelly's favorite drinks is what we normally call a French martini, but we don't do the martini glass or no-ice thing. I actually make it in a short glass with ice. Since I'm writing this for the book, I should be exact about it, and so I've changed the name to "French on the Rocks"—which in French is "Français sur les Roches." But that literally means "rocks," so maybe it should be "Français sur les Cubes de Glace," or on "the ice cubes." Well, whatever it is, it's *très bien* (damn good).

> Ice
> 2 ounces vodka
> 1 ounce pineapple juice
> Splash raspberry liqueur
> Lemon wedge

Put ice in a glass and add (in this order) the vodka, pineapple juice, and raspberry liqueur.

Don't stir—it looks kinda cool when the liqueur puddles at the bottom.

Squeeze and drop in the lemon wedge.

Hold up the glass and say aloud, "Hey, Kelly, what's up?"

Now stir and drink.

raspberry gin & tonic MAKES 1

In parts of this world, the classic gin & tonic, or "G&T" as it's often known, is the warm-weather cocktail of choice. And we've made it better by adding some raspberry liqueur.

Ice
2   ounces gin—use decent gin because cheap gin is the worst of the cheap
    alcohols to drink
    Tonic water
1   ounce raspberry liqueur
2   or 3 raspberries
    Lemon wedge

Put ice in a glass and add the gin. Fill three quarters of the way with tonic. Add the liqueur, drop in the raspberries, then squeeze and drop in the lemon. Serve.

tequila sunrise MAKES 1

Grilling makes me think of good weather, and good weather makes me think of summer, and summer makes me think of Phoenix when we lived there, and Phoenix makes me think of a place we used to eat, and that place reminds me of my friend Steve who I wish I saw more often. And I haven't had a sunrise in a while either. See, it all makes sense.

    Ice
2   ounces tequila
1   ounce orange juice
    About ½ ounce grenadine

Put ice in a glass and add the tequila and OJ.

Drizzle the grenadine slowly over the ice and watch it sink to the bottom and create the sunrise.

Ahhhhh.

cherry bourbon lemonade MAKES 1

To me, this is basically summer in a glass.

    Ice
2 **ounces lemonade**
2 **ounces bourbon**
3 **jarred maraschino cherries**
    Bamboo skewer
    Small lemon wedge

Put ice into a glass. Add the lemonade and bourbon.

Skewer 3 maraschino cherries onto a bamboo skewer and place in the glass.

Stir in 1 teaspoon of juice from the cherry jar, then squeeze and drop in the lemon wedge.

Drink.

pineapple with rum butter SERVES 6

1 **large pineapple**
¼ **cup (½ stick) butter**
¾ **cup brown sugar**
⅓ **cup dark rum**
    Ice cream, for serving

Cut the top and bottom off the pineapple, then remove the rind in long strips from the top to the bottom. Cut the pineapple into 1-inch rounds.

Preheat the grill to medium.

Put the butter, brown sugar, and rum in a small pan on the grill and stir to combine.

When the mixture starts melting, add the pineapple to the grill and, basting the whole time with the rum butter, cook the pineapple on both sides until it starts getting grill marks and is warmed all the way through.

Serve with ice cream (as if you didn't know) and any extra rum butter.

mango dessert tacos MAKES 8

Take a warm, cinny-sugared grilled tortilla, then add vanilla ice cream and diced mango, and what do you get? You get a crazy good, drippy, messy dessert you'll want every day of the year—grill or no grill.

8 flour tortillas
  Butter, softened
  Cinnamon-sugar (1 tablespoon sugar mixed with $\frac{1}{2}$ tablespoon ground cinnamon)
2 cups vanilla ice cream
2 fresh mangos, peeled and diced
  Honey
$\frac{1}{2}$ lemon
  Powdered sugar

Preheat the grill to medium.

Brush both sides of the tortillas lightly with butter and sprinkle well with cinny-sugar.

Grill the tortillas on both sides until slightly crispy and brown—remove to a serving plate.

Add $\frac{1}{4}$ cup of the ice cream to each tortilla and top with some of the diced mango. Drizzle with honey and a squeeze of lemon juice, then a sprinkle of powdered sugar.

Now just fold and eat like a taco.

Make sure the mangos are super ripe. Because a not-ripe mango will be hard and have no flavor.

pound cake s'mores SERVES 4

I know, stupid name . . . again. But it's not. Well, it is a stupid name, but I mean the food is not. The one part of the s'more that I never really dug was the graham cracker. So we just swap it for grilled pound cake and voilà—much, much better. And for ridiculous decadence, we add a whack of the GM'd whipped cream. Oh my . . .

- 4 wooden or metal skewers
- 3 dark chocolate bars, like a Hershey's Dark—see BTW
- 8 ¾-inch-thick slices pound cake, approximately 4 x 2¾ inches
- 8 marshmallows, the full-size ones
- ½ cup GM'd Whipped Cream (page 248)

Smash one chocolate bar up a bit (keeping it in the wrapper), using a food mallet or something heavy—set aside.

Preheat the grill to medium-low and remove the grates from part of the grill so you have direct access to the flame— hey, we're makin' s'mores here people!

Place all the pound cake on the grill and allow to get good grill marks on one side. Flip and add ½ chocolate bar to each of the 4 pound cake pieces.

Put 2 marshmallows on each skewer and, using the grate-removed side, cook the marshmallows over the grill flames until blackened. Place on top of the chocolate pieces and cover with another grilled piece of pound cake.

Put on a plate and sqwoosh down so the marshmallow kind of oozes out the sides of the pound cake a bit.

Add whipped cream to each and sprinkle the broken chocolate pieces over the top.

You can mess around with milk chocolate all you want on your own time, but please don't do it here. This is about dark chocolate.

grilled peaches SERVES 4

Maybe the simplest of any grilled dessert, this little gem is ideal with ice cream, if you're an ice cream person. But I think it's more amazing with the Raspberry Whipped Cream, but hey —what do I know?

- **4 ripe, but not too ripe, peaches, halved and pitted**
- **2 tablespoons butter, melted**
- **⅓ cup brown sugar**
- **½ lemon**
- **Ice Cream or Raspberry Whipped Cream (page 249), for serving**

Ice cream or Raspberry Whipped Cream (page 249), for serving

Preheat the grill to medium.

Brush the peaches with the butter and sprinkle with the brown sugar.

Grill the peaches for 3 to 4 minutes a side. Serve warm with a squeeze of the lemon juice and either ice cream or the Raspberry Whipped Cream.

whipped cream heaven

What's not to like here? Whipped cream is like the bacon of the dessert world—everything is honestly better with it.

basic everyday whipped cream

MAKES ENOUGH FOR 8 TO 10 SERVINGS

2 cups (1 pint) heavy whipping cream
1 tablespoon vanilla extract
¼ cup sugar

Combine the cream and vanilla in a bowl. Beat with an electric mixer for about a minute.

Add the sugar and continue beating for about 4 minutes, or just until the peaks form and hold their shape.

- The stuff in the can bears absolutely no resemblance to this real, "whip-it-yourself" version and should never be used (unless you're in college, and then it won't be used for food and that's okay.)

- When it's whipped enough, you should be able to hold the bowl upside down over your head and nothing will come out. Please note I said "should." If you do it wrong, it's not my fault.

- You can go too far beating the cream, and if you do, you'll end up with a gross curdled mess. Stop when it has soft, firm peaks. Did I just write that?

- You can also whip cream by hand—you just don't want to. Be prepared to stand there with a whisk beating a long, long time . . .

- Whipped cream should last for about 24 hours in the fridge—unless one of your kids finds it and puts it on everything.

- Good whipped cream is the reason to buy good, fresh berries—and vice versa.

gm'd whipped cream MAKES ENOUGH FOR 8 TO 10 SERVINGS

I love this, and the GM is sweet enough—you don't need to add sugar.

  2 **cups (1 pint) heavy whipping cream**
2-3 **tablespoons Grand Marnier**

Combine the cream and Grand Marnier in a large bowl. Beat with an electric mixer for about 4 minutes, or just until soft peaks form and hold their shape.

Now that you know how easy it is to flavor whipping cream, try more

flavors—like these:

RASPBERRY

Raspberry liqueur, like Chambord

I also like to stir in a few busted-up raspberries if I have them. It makes the

whipped cream look amazing.

COFFEE

Espresso, cold or room temp, or

Coffee liqueur

LICORICE (ANISE)

Sambuca

MINT

Fresh chopped and some mint extract

CHOCOLATE

Chocolate liqueur, or
Chocolate syrup

G.B.F. (grilled bananas foster) SERVES 4

At another show we shot at the San Diego Zoo, I made a version of this right in front of the gorilla exhibit. Was that mean of me?

2 ripe bananas, peeled and cut in half lengthwise
¼ cup (½ stick) butter, softened
⅓ cup brown sugar
¼ cup dark rum
4 scoops Ben & Jerry's Chunky Monkey ice cream
½ cup dried banana chips, crunched up a bit

Preheat the grill to medium-high.

Slice the bananas into ½-inch pieces and add them to a pan with the butter and brown sugar. Cook over medium heat until they begin to soften. Take the pan off the heat and add the rum. Gently tip the pan toward the flame—not so any liquid drips out, just so the fumes catch the fire and it starts to flame. Don't worry, it'll go out quickly. Let the whole thing just kinda do its thing and get all amazing.

Put the ice cream in a bowl, add some of the bananas, and sprinkle some of the chips over the top—eat, eat, and eat.

lemon raspberry granita MAKES ABOUT 2½ CUPS

A granita is essentially a semifrozen dessert—and the perfect thing to have when it's warm and you've been grilling.

	Grated zest (the outer yellow layer) of 2 lemons
½	cup fresh squeezed lemon juice
1½	cups water
⅓	cup sugar
1	tablespoon raspberry liqueur

Put the grated lemon zest in a saucepan with the lemon juice, water, sugar, and liqueur. Bring to a simmer, stirring until the sugar is dissolved.

Transfer the mixture to a metal bowl and put in the freezer. Stir every 30 minutes to stir up the ice that's been forming.

Continue freezing and stirring until it's slightly slushy, 3 to 4 hours, then serve it slushy in a martini glass or something clear—cuz it'll look great.

Or . . . instead of freezing in a bowl:

Once the sugar is dissolved, cool the liquid, put it into ice cube trays, and freeze until hard—at least 2 hours. Just before serving, put the cubes into a food processor and process until chunky/smooth. Serve.

grilled strawberry trifle SERVES 4

A trifle is a dessert with layers of custard (or pudding) or whipped cream, fruit, and sponge cake. It's usually made in a big pedestal glass serving bowl so you see all the pretty layers. But since I don't own one, we'll make ours on plates and they'll still be beautiful. And this one will also have grilled angel food cake for a warm, really bitchin' layer.

- 8 ½-inch slices angel food cake
- 1 cup vanilla pudding, just buy it already made
- 1 cup sliced fresh strawberries
- ½ cup Raspberry Whipped Cream (page 249)
- ⅓ cup Strawberry Sauce (see below)

Preheat the grill to medium. Grill the angel food cake on both sides until it has beautiful grill marks. This won't take long.

Then build the trifle on a plate from the bottom up like this: cake, pudding, strawberries, cake, pudding strawberries, whipped cream.

Give a final drizzle of the Strawberry Sauce over the top.

strawberry sauce MAKES ABOUT 1½ CUPS

Super simple—you can combine this with any of the whipped creams
(page 249) and any fruit and you'll be a hero. I like to put this in a plastic
container and throw it in the freezer.

16 ounces frozen unsweetened strawberries, thawed
¼ cup sugar
1 tablespoon fresh squeezed lemon juice

Place the thawed strawberries with their juice, sugar, and lemon juice in a
food processor or blender. Blend until smooth. Refrigerate for up to about
a week or freeze.

my grandma ruth's chocolate sauce
MAKES ABOUT A CUP

My Grandma Ruth was a master in the kitchen, and this is an example of
her simple perfection. We freeze what we don't use, then just microwave
to re-warm.

3 tablespoons butter
2 squares unsweetened Baker's chocolate
6 ounces evaporated milk
¾ cup sugar

Put butter and chocolate in small pot on low heat. Stir until melted.

Stir in milk and slowly add sugar.

Bring to a low boil for 2 to 3 minutes, stiffing often.

Use.

index.